"I decided to read *Connect with Your Kid* to see what I could learn that might help me with the families I work with in my private counseling practice. I found myself reading the book with my parent hat on instead. As the father of two teenagers I found the information invaluable and began using many of the communication skills described in the book. Now that my son is seventeen, I found the 'use open-ended questions' section especially helpful. This is a book that every parent should read if you want to understand your child better and effectively communicate. Bravo!!"

> —**Thomas Kersting**, Licensed psychotherapist, author of *Disconnected: How to Protect Your Kids from the Harmful Effects of Device Dependency*

"*Connect with Your Kid* is a must read for parents who want to prepare and position their children for a lifetime of success. Dr. Coates has the book jam packed with wisdom, practical examples and easy-to-implement strategies that will quickly make any parent more effective."

> —**Sam X Renick**, Children's author, award-winning financial literacy educator

"At this pivotal time when kids are changing dramatically and their independence is right around the corner, parents are often caught off guard, ill-equipped to deal with the transition from training a child to coaching an emerging adult. In this book, Dr. Coates helps us understand this context, builds our parenting self-awareness, identifies the most important communication scenarios to 'get it right,' and provides compelling examples and instruction that guide us to a flourishing adult-to-adult relationship. With empathy and wise counsel, he teaches us how to communicate in a way that will be well-received by our children, fostering mutual understanding, respect, and trust for a lifetime. A must read for every parent!"

> —**Dennis J. Trittin**, President of LifeSmart Publishing, and author of *What I Wish I Knew at 18*, *Parenting for the Launch*, and *Wings Not Strings*

"Sage advice. Listen to understand, coach your child to learn how to think, and value your child's growing autonomy. Help your young adults grow into successful social-emotionally whole humans who love themselves and respect and value others. In this time of change, parents can feel reassured by the wisdom and guidance of Dr. Dennis Coates. *Connect with Your Kid* is critically needed as parenting young adults in this digital age demands that we enhance our emotional intelligence, our communication skills, and the manner in which we express our deep caring toward those in our world. It's filled with meaningful communication strategies that are easy to use such as the FAR approach, 5 Magic Reflection Questions, and 'Listening Moments.' Get out your highlighters and post-it notes; reading this book is going to be a valuable experience for you, your family, and our community."

    —Lynne Kenney, PsyD, pediatric psychologist

"I love this book even more than *How Your Teen Can Grow a Smarter Brain*! I especially like the clear format and all the concrete examples. The quotes are great. And I like the suggestion that after tackling Listening to Understand that parents can work on the other skills in any order. Chapter 14 emphasizes the time it takes to first learn and consistently reach for a new skill."

    —Elisabeth Stitt, parenting coach and author of *Parenting as a Second Language*

"*Connect with Your Kid* provides well-informed and actionable ways for parents to get in touch with their best selves, foster a healthy life and development for their child or teenager, and strengthen the familial relationship. Households will deeply benefit from this unprecedented opportunity to improve vital parent-child communication skills."

    —Kristine Tye, MA, MFT, Licensed therapist, teen specialist and parenting coach

"This book is so easy to read and understand. It really makes you look at your parenting and realize some of the ways you are communicating with your teenagers may not be best for them, even though you mean well. I immediately put into practice changing my dialogue with my boys and saw instant results. This is a must read if you are raising teenagers. Don't we all wish they came with a manual? This is just as good!"

    —Tyse Kimball, mother of two teenage sons

"This book couldn't have come at a more perfect time. Schools shut down due to the virus and several weeks into a new way of doing things, our normally happy-go-lucky children were having challenges. They were feeling a sense of loss, missing time spent with their friends. They celebrated their birthdays in a way they'd never done before. Having never experienced anything like this before, my wife and I did the best we could to communicate with our children, but sometimes it just didn't feel like enough. Reading this book has helped us immensely and has allowed us to have far more engaging and rewarding conversations with our children. Two nights ago, we all sat at the dinner table, talking for over an hour together as a family, long after we'd all finished eating."

—**Kevin Thompson**, Founder of Tribe for Leaders and father of seven

"Yet another great book from Denny Coates—more really useful practical tips, advice and guidance to help us be even better parents, grandparents and professionals supporting teenagers."

—**Frank Thompson**, Personal/Careers Adviser at Gateway Academy, Essex, UK

"This is a book you'll want to keep close, because you'll be referring to it often. It's the perfect resource for parents who want to have honest conversations that will guide their child as they grow up as well as strengthen their relationship! Regardless of how good (or bad) your communication skills are, you'll learn ways to be more effective in this straightforward book!"

—**Cath Hakanson**, RN, Founder of Sex Ed Rescue and parent of a tween and teen

"The writing is so clear and concise, great for parents short on time. The communication skills described are relevant to other types of relationships, too, not just parents and kids. With this book, even people who already have strong communication skills can discover ways to improve."

—**Alexis Rodegerdts**, Librarian and mother of three

"*Connect with Your Kid* is a wonderful contribution to the parenting literature. A keeper! Coates helps the reader think about the big picture—how they want to communicate with their children over a lifetime. It's not about giving the right answers. It's about asking the right questions. The book describes straightforward concepts to remember in any situation, like recognizing a 'listening moment' and engaging a 'listening mindset.' The book is sophisticated yet simple at the same time. The examples of situations to expect and model conversations are so real you feel like you're living them. Coates is encouraging as he helps the reader realize that changing communication behavior, especially their own, takes time and practice, and it's worth the effort."

—**Joanie Connell**, author of *Flying without a Helicopter: How to Prepare Young People for Work and Life*

"Dr. Coates has clearly identified and explained 10 vital parent-child communication skills, in this easy-to-understand and encouraging book. He gently coaches parents to develop these skills, which will not only help them bond with their kids, but will assist the young people to think critically and problem solve. I really like his real-life examples, tips. and reminders; and the compassionate way he urges me to keep on trying even when I fall back into old patterns which don't serve me or my family."

—**Karen McFadyen**, Ph.D., researcher and mother of two teenagers

Connect with Your Kid

Connect with Your Kid

Mastering the Top 10 Parent-Child
Communication Skills

Dennis E. Coates, Ph.D.

First Summit Publishing

1st
Summit
Publishing

Connect with Your Kid: Mastering the Top 10 Parent-Child Communication Skills

Printed in the United States of America
Published by First Summit Publishing
An imprint of Performance Support Systems, Inc.
757-873-3700

Requests to publish work from this book should be sent to:
DrDennyCoates@gmail.com

Cover and book design: Paula Schlauch

ISBN: 978-1-7348051-3-0

Quantity sales. Special discounts are available on quantity purchases by corporations, associations and others. For details, contact us at info@growstrongleaders.com or 757-656-4765.

For Brooke, Stafford, Piru and Parker, who are giving their best every day to raise five terrific kids.

Contents

Preface

Most parents love their kids beyond measure, but few have strong communication skills. As a result, parents sometimes don't handle confrontations well. In your child's halting, unpredictable steps towards maturity, they may say or do things that disappoint or hurt your feelings. These clashes can make a tough day a lot worse. You might feel shock, frustration or anger. Volatile emotions could trigger yelling, arguing, or punishment. While these are natural reactions, children who are learning who they are and discovering independence might further distance themselves from you. The consequence can be resentment and distrust, leading eventually to a defiant young adult who gets in trouble and whose reactive pattern of communicating doesn't serve them well in adulthood.

If anything like this is happening, you'll have a hard time connecting for some of the many heart-to-heart talks your child needs. There will be fewer moments for teaching life skills, sharing wisdom, or encouraging activities that lead to growing up smart, happy and successful. In short, a pattern of reacting emotionally can fracture your best hopes for your child.

This book is about the solution: improving 10 parent-child communication skills that, if used consistently and with compassion, will draw your child closer to you, not push them away. These skills are:

- Listening to understand

- Coaching kids to think for themselves

- Guiding learning from experience

- Getting buy-in for expectations

- Offering encouragement
- Expressing appreciation
- Giving feedback constructively
- Accepting feedback graciously
- Engaging in dialogue
- Resolving conflict creatively

There are many more interpersonal skills than these ten. However, I've been helping adults improve their communication skills for over 40 years; and in my opinion, these are the most basic, frequently used skills. They're the ones that deliver the greatest impact—my "Top 10" for parents. Each skill consists of essential elements, or subskills. As with mastering any skill, the goal is to establish a habit for using them. And to do that, you'll need to use them repeatedly over time. You may sometimes forget or make mistakes, but you can learn from these lapses as you gradually connect the brain cells involved into physical circuits.

Learning any skills, such as those needed for an art form or a sport, will take time and effort. You can learn to paint or play golf on your own, but it helps to have a teacher or coach to keep you focused on the fundamentals.

I've structured this book to be a helpful coaching resource. Each of the 10 skill chapters:

- Describes the essential elements of the skill
- Explains why they're important
- Gives examples, tips, and reminders
- Encourages you to stay the course until the skill feels natural and automatic.

- Summarizes the main points of the chapter

- Gives suggestions for further reading

Part One describes the magnitude of the opportunity. It explains the changes that happen at puberty, how parents often react to issues instinctively, and why this reactivity is destructive to the parent-child relationship. It affirms the benefit of preparing for this phase of parenting well in advance, then goes into detail about how to master a communication skill (or any skill, for that matter).

Part Two is your skill coaching reference. I always advise parents to begin working on listening first. In relationships, you need to use listening more often than any other skill, and it's often a component of the other skills. Before attempting to learn these other skills, I suggest you stick with practicing the elements of listening until they start to feel natural and automatic. Any coach will tell you: *You gotta get your reps.*

After mastering listening, you can choose to work on any of the other skills next, and you don't need to take them in sequence. Learning to be an effective listener and mastering the other skills will take time. Like improving your serve in tennis or baking a better croissant, becoming the best parent you can be will be a journey. If you use this book to discover the skills, commit to applying them with your kids, work through discouragement, and learn from your mistakes, becoming a better communicator is definitely doable. And if you work at it, you can continue to improve for the rest of your life.

The secret: *Don't give up.*

Dennis E. Coates, Ph.D.

PART ONE

....

Three Things You Need to Know

When I was in middle school, I decided I wanted to play golf. I got the best clubs I could afford, and I studied the best books about golf. However, on the golf course I confronted reality: Golf is a hard game, and there's no substitute for a good teacher, lots of practice, and the patience to learn from experience. I was motivated to work at it, though, and I eventually became a decent player.

The basic elements of communicating one-on-one effectively aren't complicated. It takes time to replace old habits, which by now are hard-wired in your brain. But if you're committed to applying what you learn in this book, you can persist until the skills become habitual. Millions of people have done it, and so can you.

To sustain your commitment and feed your success, start by appreciating three things:

- The way you communicate with a small child won't serve you well during the second dozen years of growing up.

- The natural tendency to exercise parental authority can get in your way of communicating effectively.

- The first step to mastering communication skills is to understand how skill-building works.

"Adolescents are not monsters. They are just people trying to learn how to make it among the adults in the world, who are probably not so sure themselves."

Virginia Satir

1

....

Puberty Changes the Game

I sometimes refer to adolescence as "the second dozen years of growing up." For me, a lot of water has flowed under the bridge since I was that young. How about you? Do you remember what it was like to be a teenager?

Several years ago, I had a reunion with some high school buddies I hadn't seen in nearly 50 years. It was an amazing experience and a lot of fun. I remember one comment my old friend Brian made about me: "Coates, you were always up to something. I never knew what you'd do next." He was talking about mischief, not science projects. I thought it was an odd thing to say, and I didn't know what to make of it. A lot of time had passed since I was a freshman in high school—an inconceivable amount of life experience, learning, and change. I'm not at all the same person Brian knew back then.

A few years after the reunion, I began writing about adolescent development, a topic that has become my passionate interest. Along the way I did the memory work to recall my own teen journey. And to my surprise, I concluded that indeed, I had been a trouble-maker!

On the one hand, I had an impressive resume for such a young teen. I worked two jobs. I was the only student in my school who made straight A's. I was an Eagle Scout. I attended church three times a week.

But I cut up in class a lot. You might even say I was disruptive. In science class my buddy Dick (who was also at the reunion) and I used to sit in the back of the room and draw *Mad Magazine* cartoons and compete with each other to catch flies. We'd grab them out of the air, mark a score sheet, and then turn them loose. One day we hid in the storage closet and tried to hypnotize each other. On another occasion, we persuaded the science teacher, who had a fine singing voice, to sing pop tunes for us. I think I paid attention to his instruction only 10% of the time. Amazingly, in spite of my shenanigans, my teacher considered me his best student and gave me an A. But when I think about how hard I made his job, I feel regret.

And that was the least of my misdeeds. I did other things that were destructive and against the law. I won't go into the details because to tell you the truth, I'm embarrassed to even think about it. Just take my word for it. I had a secret life that could have launched me on a pathway towards trouble. The more I remember about my early teens, I have to admit that yes, Brian was right. I was always up to something.

But why? I can only give the strange answer that teenagers still give to this day: "I don't know." Like most adolescents, I made a lot of my decisions impulsively. My pranks seemed like something fun to do at the time, and I gave no thought to the consequences. That's one of the perils of the teen journey: kids sometimes do dumb things for no good reason.

Puberty marks the beginning of adolescence. It's the onset of hormonal activity that triggers a spurt of physical growth and maturation of reproductive organs. Typically, this begins in girls (10-12) before boys (11-13). With girls, the most dramatic indication is the first menstrual cycle, which arrives a couple years after puberty begins. With boys, signs are more gradual and less noticeable.

The timing of these changes varies considerably from child to child. As a result, a parent can suddenly realize that their child is slowly becoming an adult, when in fact this process may have been going on for years. Puberty usually happens before a child "officially" becomes a teenager. And adolescence, which begins at the onset of puberty, involves a process of brain growth that lasts beyond the teen years into the early twenties.

The physical changes, while gradual, are monumental. One of the major consequences is the sexual aspect: a pre-teen gains the ability to reproduce. This is vastly important. The persistence of the human species—indeed the viability of any species—depends on its ability to reproduce. In modern times, the desire of an adolescent child to get involved in sex happens many years before they are ready for the responsibilities of raising a child.

Perhaps even more important are the consequences of mental maturation. Every teenager will eventually grow into their adult bodies. Good nutrition and physical activity can influence this development somewhat, but mostly the end result is driven by genetics.

Not so with brain development. While most areas of the brain are fully developed before puberty, one important exception is the prefrontal cortex (PFC). I often refer to the PFC as "the smart part of the brain," because it handles self-regulation, conceptual learning, evaluation, reasoning, problem-solving, decision-making, planning, organizing, and self-discipline—some amazing thinking skills that empower success as an adult.

At puberty, growth hormones trigger a second wave of PFC development. Each brain cell in the PFC then blossoms with hundreds of new connector fibers (dendrites). This process prepares the PFC for connecting its cells into circuits for the various kinds of cognitive capacity needed for adult life. However, as in learning any skill, a child will have to exercise them repeatedly for the circuits to form.

This means two things: (1) A child will have to apply these skills repeatedly to develop this part of the brain, and (2) Each child will develop a different capacity for adult thinking, because not every child will make the same effort. Therefore, each child will be acquiring a different set of critical thinking skills at a time when they're pushing for more independence.

This is why parent-child communication is so important. The problem is, only a few fortunate parents have had training in communication skills. Without these skills, the natural tendency is to react to parent-child confrontations with a mixture of emotion and parental authority. The unfortunate consequence can be a diminishment of respect and trust and further distancing of the child from the parent, often leading to defiance. This can fracture your ability to guide and nurture your adolescent child. If a weak sense of self is combined with peer pressure, a young person could get involved in risky or thrill-seeking activities. If judgment is poorly developed, a teen could fall prey to any of the many perils of adolescence:

- Alcohol/drug abuse or addiction
- Addiction to pornography, gaming, social networking
- Sexual predators
- Rape
- Pregnancy
- Sexually transmitted infections
- Bullying
- Breaking the law
- Gangs
- Traffic accidents
- Low self-esteem, peer pressure, and conformity
- Unrelieved stress and depression

- Self-harming or suicide
- Alienation and defiance
- Running away from home
- Sex trafficking
- Sleep deprivation
- Eating disorders
- Academic failure
- Poor work ethic
- Failure to launch

I probably left out some of the scarier outcomes; but still, it's a long list. Aside from addiction, one of the dangers of alcohol/drug abuse and excessive screen time is that they cause chemicals to enter the PFC that can suppress cognitive development during adolescence—a horrible and poorly understood consequence.

On the other hand, adolescence can be a wonderful period in your child's life. They can get involved in satisfying activities that lead to becoming a happy, successful, independent adult:

- Become an avid reader
- Study hard and become knowledgeable and well-informed
- Learn how to learn
- Build critical thinking skills
- Get involved in service projects
- Become passionately interested in things that could lead to a career
- Set goals for the future

- Get a job and save money for college
- Develop a strong work ethic
- Maintain healthy nutrition and physical fitness habits
- Spend time out in nature
- Become responsible and independent
- Learn practical life skills
- Earn strong self-esteem and self-confidence
- Develop empathy, compassion, and sensitivity
- Improve relationship and leadership skills
- Make friendships that last a lifetime
- Have a lot of good, wholesome fun
- Strengthen bonds with parents and siblings
- Choose their own path of spirituality
- Get accepted by a branch of the military, a good trade school or college, prepared to do next-level work

Again, avoiding the gauntlet of dangers and pursuing the many positive aspects of growing up depend in large part on your child's developing good judgment—wiring the PFC for a variety of critical thinking skills. You can do a lot to encourage and support this development. I've described the practical possibilities in my book, *How Your Teen Can Grow a Smarter Brain*.

But sharing wisdom, teaching life skills, encouraging your child to use good judgment, and other ways of helping them prepare for adult life depend on whether you've built a bridge of communication. They need to be willing to consider your input. Using effective communication skills is the key to growing the bond between you and your adolescent child, so they welcome your wisdom and encouragement.

As you'll learn in Chapter 3, improving these vital skills takes time. Ideally, you'll begin this effort well before your child reaches puberty, so you're able to use the skills confidently when they're most needed. But it's never too late to change the game; you can make a huge difference by becoming a better communicator while your child is a teenager.

This chapter in a nutshell:

- **Realistically, adolescence is a time when a lot of wonderful things can happen—or a lot of awful things.**

- **Your ability to influence positive adolescent development depends on whether you're connecting with their child—using vital communication skills.**

- **Ideally, you'll begin working on your communication skills during the years before a child reaches adolescence.**

Learn more about building parent-child relationships:

- Thomas Gordon, *Parent Effectiveness Training* (Three Rivers, 2000)

- Dennis Coates, *How Your Teen Can Grow a Smarter Brain*, 2nd Ed. (First Summit, 2020)

"An adolescent does not rebel against her parents. She rebels against their power. If parents would rely less on power and more on nonpower methods to influence their children from infancy on, there would be little for children to rebel against when they become adolescents. The use of power to change the behavior of children, then, has this severe limitation: parents inevitably run out of power, and sooner than they think."

Thomas Gordon

2

....

Reactivity: How Your Instincts Let You Down

As a parent, you hold all the high cards: size, strength, wisdom, skill, experience, money, and authority. Did I forget something? Even though you may love your child beyond all reason, it's your house and your rules; and you have the clout to enforce them. You're the law.

Your child knows this. Their entire history as a child up to this point is colored by their dependency on you. They have only a dim understanding of how the world works. They're not even sure who they are; their earnest quest for an individual identity won't begin until adolescence. In desperation, they may try to push your buttons, but you can win every argument or conflict.

This assessment of your power paints a severe and dreary picture. Not that you'll play the power cards in every situation. You may exercise compassion and understanding as a general rule. But when exhausted, have you ever been tempted to say, "Because I said so"?

It would only be natural if you did. Human beings are rational, far more so than any other species on Earth. But we're also an emotional species. When it seems as though everything in your day is one more challenge, one more assault on your equilibrium, the desire to shout or strike back is a natural emotional reaction. You may react to the surprising and irrational behavior of your child with shock, dismay, frustration, disappointment, and even anger. But kids have always resented being treated this way, even if later in life they move on and forgive their parents. It's an old story.

Instinctive reactions take many forms. Here are some of the more hurtful ones.

Orders, commands, warnings, threats, and ultimatums

You want X but your kid wants Y, which is unacceptable to you. You own the car, the house, and practically everything in it. You even own your teen's precious smartphone. To get your way, you can play the power card.

"I don't care if you're tired of doing the dishes. Get in there and do it."

"I won't have you going to school looking like a tramp. Go upstairs and change into something appropriate."

"Turn that awful music down."

"For the hundredth time, don't slam the door."

"If you come home late one more time, I'll ground you for the rest of the year."

"Just so you understand: you get just one moving violation and I'll take away the car keys for good."

The message: *While you're still living under this roof, you'll do what I say.* My wife once told me that her father used to say, *"When I say 'jump,' you say 'how high' on the way up."* Directives like this come from the inherent power and authority parents have over their kids. Exercising parental authority doesn't promote a loving, sharing relationship. At a time when teenagers are seeking more independence, they want the understanding and respect normally given to adults. So naturally they resent the autocratic approach, in which they're treated as if they're still little kids. They might even become defiant and rebellious.

You may not intend to convey this sentiment, but it's encoded in the approach to parent-child communication that's been handed down from generation to generation. The problem is, teenagers don't want to be controlled; and ordering them around is a good way to erode the relationship. If you talked to other adults this way, you'd have big problems.

Criticism, blame, shame, ridicule, insults, and sarcasm

Most teenagers resist this kind of verbal attack, because it implies they lack intelligence and can't figure things out for themselves. There are two possible reactions, both damaging to young people. They may resent their parents and brush off the verbal abuse. Or they might give credence to what their parents say and suffer damage to their self-esteem.

"That attitude will get you nowhere."

"That was a dumb thing to do."

"It's your own fault."

"It's no wonder you're in such a mess."

"Don't be such a whiner."

"Oh that was cute. Nice move."

"You should be ashamed of yourself."

"The problem is, you're lazy."

"If you want to be treated like an adult, then act like one."

Comments that imply a child is inadequate, incompetent, inept, incapable, or unworthy have the power to erode their self-esteem.

Lecturing, preaching, debating, arguing, and giving advice

Most parents have learned enough about life to believe they know what's best for their kids, and they feel they're being helpful when they tell their kids what they should do. It can be hard to watch your child struggle with a difficult situation. You have wisdom and experience, and you may feel that giving an answer or a solution can relieve anxiety and maybe teach something.

"Here's what you need to tell your teacher...."

"That's not the way you act in this house."

"I think you're taking on too much."

"Let me tell you what's going on here."

"There's a lot better way to handle this."

Helping, solving, fixing, and giving advice—all with a loving heart. You probably do, in fact, know best. But as kids get older, this kind of lecturing can send a demeaning message: *I'm smarter than you are, you're naïve, you're wrong, you don't know what you're doing, you'll fail without my help.*

When you take over your child's problems, you rob them of the opportunity to practice thinking and coping skills; and you promote dependence at a time when they should be learning independence. Young people become problem solvers by solving problems, and they gain self-confidence by achieving things through their own efforts. If they're to prepare themselves for adult life, they'll need plenty of experience working through problems.

Physical attacks

Sometimes a parent's frustration and anger can be so intense that they react with physical violence. While not intended, an attack can cause injury. Even if it doesn't, such a reaction can provoke fear and resentment, which could damage the parent-child relationship, if not the kid's emotional well-being.

When I was 10 years old, my family visited my maternal grandparents in McGill, Nevada. Mom was the eighth of sixteen children, and three of my aunts were still living at home. The youngest, Janey, who was three years older than I, was taller, stronger, and wiser. One morning, she and I were playing in the living room. Our contest reached a physical stage and she grabbed me from behind. I turned hard to free myself and she fell to the floor. In one motion, my grandmother leaned forward, lifted her massive weight out of her chair and slapped me as hard as she could across my face.

"You don't shove girls," she said with a frown and fell back into her chair.

I was on the floor, the left side of my face hot and stinging. Surprised and stunned, I struggled to keep from crying. "We were just playing. I didn't hurt her," I said.

She gave me a cold look. She didn't appreciate this challenge to her authority. "I don't care. Don't ever do it again."

I turned my head towards the living room window, a blaze of white light. I didn't want to look at my grandmother's face, and I didn't look at her again during that visit. When the family left, I didn't say goodbye to her; and we never returned to McGill. I never saw my grandmother again, and I never again thought of her with affection.

I was the oldest of eight kids. My own parents, who were loving and devoted to our well-being, rarely resorted to physical forms of discipline. I remember that my dad sometimes reacted to one of my unruly siblings with the threat, "You cut that out right now or I'll knock you into next week." I never understood what this would look like because he never followed through; apparently the threat was effective enough.

The bottom line is that while my parents were doing the best they could to raise a large family under sometimes difficult circumstances, they didn't have effective communication skills. I don't fault them for this. Practically no parent of their generation had considered improving the way they communicate. Most of them learned how to raise kids from the example of their own parents. Later, as a parent myself, I wasn't aware of the concept of effective communication, either. My mastery of these essential skills would come later.

Once when I was a young parent, I was driving the family into town, and my two sons began fighting in the back seat. I yelled a firm command to stop fighting, but they ignored me. This caused me to lose my temper. I took a wild swing at the back seat, missing both boys. The car veered right, almost leaving the road. I was furious. Thankfully, the boys' mother dealt with the situation. It's not a memory I'm proud of.

Toxic questions

The questions parents ask can hurt, too. Sometimes name-calling and put-downs are implied in the questions they ask. As someone who has written extensively about raising kids, I'm now far more aware of what helps and what doesn't. But back in the late 70s, I wasn't what you would call a conscious parent. I'm sure that from time to time I said something like *"What's wrong with you?"* or *"Can't you follow simple instructions?"*

These are what I call *toxic questions*.

"What's wrong with you?" is something a frustrated parent might say when their child has done something they've been asked not to do—for the umpteenth time. The question implies a hurtful message: *You're flawed as a person. You're too dumb to do what's right, even after you've been told. There's something wrong with you.*

Or in a tired, overwhelmed moment a parent might say in a raised voice: "Why did you do that?" The question has no answer. No child knows why they sometimes do inappropriate things. But the question carries a hidden message: *What you did is so stupid that I can't imagine why you, or anyone for that matter, would do that. You're incompetent.*

A regular diet of hidden messages like these may be indistinguishable from psychological abuse. Here are a few other common toxic messages:

"What do you think you're doing?"

"What on Earth were you thinking?"

"How many times do I have to tell you...?"

"What am I going to do with you?"

"Why don't you do what you're told?"

"What's your problem?"

Adults who ask questions like these don't expect answers. Instead, they're sending messages. In your growing up, did any adult ever fire one of these zingers at you? How did it make you feel?

I realize now that such questions strike at the heart of a child's self-esteem. So why did I say them? I may have said them because I felt tired and frustrated at the time; I didn't appreciate their hidden meaning; and they were probably things my own parents used to say when they were tired and frustrated.

Still, toxic questions can damage a kid's self-worth. During the first dozen years of growing up, most kids think their parents are perfect. Parents seem to know everything, while kids know relatively little about anything. So when they're assaulted by the hidden message that there's something wrong with them, it's difficult for a young person to repudiate it. After being on the receiving end of enough of these questions, a child's self-esteem can erode.

One of the consequences of weak self-esteem during the second dozen years of growing up is being vulnerable to peer pressure. Unsure of themselves and desperate to be liked by their peers, they could get involved in harmful or even tragic behavior.

Reacting emotionally can be destructive. When you, the all-powerful source of love and safety, lash out, a child can become afraid or less trusting. An older child might feel anger or lose respect for the parent. The consequences over time can be a gradual distancing between parent and child, not the bonding you hope for.

Parents often ask what they can do to keep from yelling. A child disappoints, disobeys, or says something hurtful, and you raise your voice. Or worse. This natural, automatic reaction usually elevates the emotional quality of the situation and can leave you feeling inadequate. This isn't the kind of parent you want to be. Like me, you wish you could play those scenes over again.

Improving parent-child communication skills is a game-changer. The first step is to appreciate that your natural emotional reactivity can have negative consequences. The second step is to catch yourself when you feel your emotions boiling up. Then remember to do the hard thing, the more effective thing: *resist the impulse to express these emotions, calm yourself, and consider communicating effectively.*

The top 10 parent-child communication skills

While there are dozens of interpersonal communication skills, Part Two of this book focuses on the 10 skills that I feel give parents the greatest positive impact:

Listening to understand. Resist the impulse to talk, and start paying attention. Express empathy, and check what you think your child is trying to say. The goal is to get the message, even if the child has trouble expressing it, and even if it's something you didn't want to hear.

Coaching your child to think. Instead of lecturing, instructing or giving advice, ask open-ended questions that get your child to think. Encouraging your child to do their own thinking is the No. 1 way you can maximize their ability to learn self-regulation, good judgment, problem-solving, and decision-making.

Guiding learning from experience. Successes, as well as mistakes and failures, happen all the time. Ideally, your child learns from these experiences; but this doesn't always happen. You can help them reflect on what has happened to learn lessons that will prepare them for life.

Getting buy-in for expectations. The traditional approach is to expect kids to do what you tell them to do. You'll get a lot more enthusiasm for compliance if you involve them in setting goals, objectives, and behavior standards.

Offering encouragement. Inevitably, your child will experience an unexpected setback. When it happens, it can cause them to lose heart or give up. A strong child may recover quickly and drive on, but not everyone is so resilient. Encouragement is the cure, if done effectively.

Expressing appreciation. Everyone wants their best efforts to be noticed and appreciated, including children. As often as possible, when your child does something well, mention the specific behaviors that pleased you. Do this more often than reacting to what disappointed you. Any sign of positive feedback is welcome, but there's a simple approach to having maximum impact.

Giving feedback constructively. First acknowledge the positives in their behavior, then describe specifically the behavior that troubled you, and why. Then describe the behavior you'd rather see. Give encouragement, and affirm your confidence that your kid can meet these expectations.

Accepting feedback graciously. Criticism rarely feels good, and even constructive feedback intended to encourage can cause a negative reaction. But feedback from your family is worth its weight in gold, and you don't want to discourage it by reacting badly. There are techniques for accepting it graciously.

Engaging in dialogue. Ask for your child's opinion, and listen to understand without debating or criticizing. You don't have to accept their reasoning, but you can learn what your child is thinking and even share your own point of view without trying to convince them that you're right.

Resolving conflict creatively. The idea is to hear what your child wants, then find out why—the needs that are driving your child's wants. Check to be sure you understand correctly. After describing your own needs, get creative: together with your child explore alternatives that will meet your needs and your kid's needs at the same time.

The primary goal of parenting is to help your child prepare for adult life. To accomplish this, you'll need the kind of relationship that will allow you to talk about important issues, share wisdom, and teach life skills. And you want this relationship to grow throughout adolescence. When a child feels understood, respected, and supported, it has an amazing impact on the relationship.

The purpose of this chapter has been to offer an alternative to the classic parental reactions to the normal irritations of family life, which tend to *tear kids down, instead of building them up*. The alternative—the difference-maker—is effective communication.

The chapters in Part Two explain what you need to do to work on becoming proficient at these skills. As you work on improving the way you communicate, there are a few things you need to keep in mind about building skills.

This chapter in a nutshell:

- **It's natural to feel annoyed, irritated, or worse when your child disappoints you.**

- **The instinctive response is to express these negative emotions.**

- **Because of your position of strength and authority, you may feel that this kind of reaction is typical and expected.**

- **Communicating negatively attacks kids' self-esteem and motivation.**

- **To build your child's sense of self and strengthen your relationship, the answer is to use a number of positive, empowering communication skills.**

Learn more about strengthening your parent-child relationship:

- Neil D. Brown, Ending the Parent-Teen Control Battle (New Harbinger, 2016)

- Thomas Gordon, *Parent Effectiveness Training* (Three Rivers/Crown, 2000)

"If you want to get good at anything where real-life performance matters, you have to actually practice that skill in context. Study, by itself, is never enough."

Josh Kaufman

3

....

The Secret to Improving Communication Skills

In Part Two you'll be encouraged to use 10 powerful communication skills with your child while addressing issues about boundaries, privileges, chores, money, friends, sex, substance abuse, homework, and life after high school, to name a few of the more important "talks." How you handle these discussions could help your child deal with problems, learn life skills, and build the kind of core strengths they'll need to be mature adults.

In the next 10 chapters, I introduce you to these skills and launch you on the journey to mastering them. Along the way, you'll discover that these aren't special parent-teen skills. They're adult-adult best practices—the same skills you could be using with your spouse, family, friends and coworkers. That's why they work so well with young people: you're communicating with them on an adult level, which is something they want.

No adult likes to be discounted or talked down to. They don't like being told what to do. They don't like it when people push their agenda instead of hearing what others have to say. They resist people who disregard their needs. Children are no different, especially as they get older. When you use adult-level communication skills with your child on a regular basis, some wonderful things can happen:

- By connecting with your child, the bond between you will grow stronger. As a consequence, you'll have more influence. If you're listening to them, they'll want to listen to you. It's a matter of mutual respect. You may even end up being one of those lucky parents whose child, when they leave home to make a life, still has a great relationship with their parents.

- Your child's self-esteem will grow. When you talk to them like an adult, you don't send the unspoken message that they're inferior in some way. Kids learn to be adults not by being treated like kids, but by striving in situations that allow them to act like adults.

- You'll have a far greater chance of avoiding the typical issues and horror stories of adolescent life, because you'll more readily find solutions to the problems that come up during the teen years.

- When you use the skills in your daily interactions, you'll be modeling the best ways of communicating. Kids learn a lot by observing their parents, and you'll be setting an example of how to communicate effectively—and how to be a great parent. You'll be investing in their future success and happiness.

- You'll be encouraging your child to exercise critical thinking and coaching them to solve problems. It's the main thing you control that will help them develop a superior mind.

As you'll see, the skills aren't complicated. But there's a "catch." *Mastering them requires a lot of practical application.* Learning about them—reading the chapters—is a great beginning. You'll become familiar with how they work and appreciate what they can do for you. And if you use them with your child on a regular basis, you'll eventually make them your automatic, habitual way of communicating.

How to rewire your brain for a new skill

When you improve a communication skill, in effect you're replacing a bad habit with a good one. It's the same process that an athlete uses to adopt a different, more effective technique; when someone gives up smoking; or when someone changes the way they eat.

After you learn what you need to do, getting to the point where you can do it well and do it consistently is a journey. If you want to improve the way you communicate with your child, you'll need to make it a habit—one that supersedes the old one.

There's a general misconception about learning a skill. Most people think that if you read the best book about it or go to an outstanding training course, value what you've learned, and even practice simulated exercises, you'll be able to change the way you do things in your life. Almost everyone thinks this is how it works, and I wish it were true. But it's not. Changing a lifelong behavior pattern takes more than having good intentions and knowing what do. While learning a better way to interact with your child is a great beginning, your challenge will be to *consistently apply* what you've learned—to actually use the skill over and over in daily interactions.

Knowing how to do something and actually doing it aren't the same thing.

The skill-building process for acquiring these skills is exactly like that of an athlete who's trying to master a better way of shooting a free-throw or hitting a tennis ball backhand with top-spin. After you've been shown what to do, you need practice, practice, and more practice.

Each "rep" stimulates the brain cells involved in the skill to continue growing towards each other until they're connected in a circuit. Further practice physically reinforces the circuit; myelin—which acts like insulation for an electric wire—surrounds the brain cells in the circuit. This allows electrochemical impulses to travel through the circuit at very high speeds. This process is why it takes so much practice to turn a skill into a habit— a comfortable, automatic behavior pattern.

And the skill needs to become a habit, because most of your interactions with your child won't be driven by conscious decisions to communicate a certain way. In the flow of a busy day, you'll need to react with the skill automatically. With enough application in the real world, the skill will eventually start to feel natural. When it does, you'll have replaced your old habitual way of reacting with a new, improved one.

People replace bad habits with better ones all the time.

Recently, I spent some time with two of my guy friends. They're very different people, but with one striking similarity: both have always been significantly overweight and have diabetes. And even though he tried, one hasn't been able to change the lifestyle that's causing his health problems. The other persisted, and in a year's time he lost 50 pounds and no longer has to take medications for diabetes.

How do you change habits like that, when your brain is already physically wired to produce the problem behavior? It took years of repetitions to create the brain circuits for the parenting habits you have now. So naturally it will take a lot of "reps" to rewire the circuits for new skills. At first you'll fight your old habit. In your everyday interactions, you'll will yourself to remember what you learned and then concentrate on doing it that way instead. You'll pick yourself up from your mistakes and failures and keep trying. Like an athlete trying to improve skills, you'll do the work.

I'm telling you this because when you read the next 10 chapters, you'll realize how powerful your conversations with your child can be. You'll "get it," and you'll be excited about what you're learning. It's important to be patient, though, and accept that changing the way you communicate can take months. Mastering all 10 skills—one at a time—could take years. It will depend on how many "reps" you're getting—how often you actually use the skills with your child.

It's helpful to think that an old, ingrained habit is like following a familiar, well-traveled road—how you usually get from Point A to Point B. You've used this route for so many years that the turns and stops are practically automatic. At some point, you realize that even though you feel like you could drive it in your sleep, the twists and turns are slowing you down and causing wear and tear on your vehicle. Like this old road, your habitual way of reacting causes problems for you and others.

And then one day you realize your journey will be far better if you have a more direct route. The better way to get to where you want to go will benefit you in lots of ways, but at first the more effective route will be under construction. In the early stages, the going will sometimes be slow and confusing. But after the expressway is finished, your journey from Point A to Point B will be faster and safer. The old route will still be there; but you'll stop using it, and eventually it will fall into disrepair.

It takes work to break a bad habit, but people do it all the time. Motivation helps. The process is easier if you understand how behavior change usually happens. This description of four stages of competence is adapted from Prochaska & DiClemente's "Transtheoretical Model":

1. **Unconscious incompetence.** Your habitual way of doing something doesn't work very well, but you aren't

aware that it's causing problems or that there's a better way.

2. **Conscious incompetence.** If you're lucky, you'll discover that what you're doing is causing issues. Maybe your behavior causes distress or problems in your relationships. Maybe someone has given you feedback. You haven't committed to change yet, but you're not blissfully unaware anymore.

3. **Conscious competence.** In this stage you learn what you should be doing instead, and you make an effort to change. At first, you have to concentrate in order to do something different. You haven't rewired your brain, so the new way isn't a habit yet. This is challenging because the old way is still an ingrained habit, still affecting your behavior. Knowledge and skills are stored as physical circuits in the brain. There's no delete switch; old habits are physically wired in your brain, so the circuits won't just disconnect themselves and go away. The trick is to repeat the new behavior so many times that your brain rewires itself for a new, more rewarding habit. This new construction takes work. At first, you know what to do and you want to do it; but sometimes you forget. A situation happens and you react automatically with your old, comfortable habit. When you realize your mistake later, you feel frustrated and discouraged. Or as you try focusing on one aspect of the skill, you overlook others. At this point you might blame the skill. You might rationalize that it just doesn't feel right. It's too hard. It's not going to work for you. You'll be tempted to give up.

4. **Unconscious competence.** If instead of giving up, you push past your lapses and consciously keep trying, each effort will stimulate the brain cells to connect, and after a while your success rate will improve. You'll still

have occasional shortfalls; but if you don't give up, if you keep trying, eventually your brain will wire itself for the new habit. This means that doing the right thing will begin to kick in automatically without a conscious effort on your part. The new behavior will become *the* way you perform the skill.

This process is how skills are built and habits are formed—both good ones and bad ones. In the past, you probably formed most of your habits without realizing you were doing so. To change them, you'll need to be self-aware—and persistent. You'll need to do the work.

The initial rough going happens to everybody. The secret for success is actually quite simple. Even though your initial failures may be disheartening, accept that they're an inevitable part of the skill development process. And *don't give up.* You'll have some successes initially, and they will happen more frequently if you learn from your experiences and continue using the skills.

The most effective way to learn from experience is the Focus-Action-Reflection (FAR) approach:

- **Focus.** Work on improving one skill at a time. You have a lot going on in your life, and working on one of the skills takes a fair amount of concentration and effort. Trying to improve more than one skill simultaneously will cause you to dilute your efforts.

- **Action.** Once you understand what's involved in a skill, getting good at it means actually doing it, over and over. Practice, practice, and more practice.

- **Reflection.** In spite of best intentions, at first you'll miss opportunities to apply what you learned; and even if you do remember, you may not do it very well. By reflecting on your experiences, you can turn these shortfalls into motivation and learning.

The five magic reflection questions

Experience can be a great teacher, but people don't always learn from their mistakes. Sometimes they go from one unfortunate experience to another without learning a thing. For maximum learning, after a successful interaction or one that didn't go well, take the time to answer these questions, in this order:

1. **What happened?** The details of an event need to be recalled in order to make sense of them. What was the sequence of events? What did you do? How did others react? How do you feel about it?

2. **Why did you handle it this way?** Things happen for a reason. To imagine a better way to handle a situation like this, try to understand why things occurred the way they did. What were you thinking? What helped or hindered? What led to the outcome?

3. **What were the consequences?** Appreciating the impact of what happened creates the motivation to handle situations like this more effectively. Benefits? Costs? Problems? Resolutions?

4. **How would you handle a similar situation in the future?** What did you learn from this experience? What basic principles? How are you going to apply the lesson?

5. **What are your next steps?** What will you do in the next 48 hours to set you up for implementing this learning?

Tips for optimum skill-building:

- **Record the lesson.** When reflecting on your mistakes, instead of just thinking about the answers to these questions, write them down. People think more thoroughly when they write, and having a record of your thoughts will allow you to review them later.

- **Persist.** In the beginning, it may seem as if you're having more failures than successes. Don't let this discourage you. Occasional lapses are par for the course. They happen to everybody, even elite athletes. Just keep trying, and your success rate will gradually improve. The secret is simply to *refuse to give up*. Remember that if you give up, your chance to improve the way you connect with your child and reap the many benefits is lost.

- **Acknowledge improvement.** When you do remember to try the new way and experience some success, give yourself credit. Be conscious of your success rate, so you know that progress is happening.

- **Get coaching.** It's hard to make it through the rewiring process without someone to encourage you to keep trying. It makes a big difference to have someone who cares enough about your success to listen to your frustrations, give feedback, encourage you, and hold you accountable. Over the long haul, this kind of support will help you work past discouragement and ingrain the new behaviors. The best coach for a parent is a spouse, because both of you can observe each other's behavior on a daily basis, and you can coach each other. Ideally your spouse will read this book along with you and embark on a similar journey to improve communication. If this isn't possible, another parent can learn with you, help you set goals, encourage you, and hold you accountable. And of course, if it's in your budget, you can work with a professional parent coach.

With enough successful encounters with your child, the new way will start to feel natural. Once you notice that you don't have to concentrate to do it, and using the skill feels comfortable and automatic, you'll have rewired your brain. You'll "own" the new skill.

This realistic perspective on adopting new behavior patterns will help you master the game-changing ways to talk to your child. They're described in the next 10 chapters, beginning with the foundation skill: *listening to understand.*

This chapter in a nutshell:

- **Knowing what to do and actually doing it aren't the same thing.**

- **Changing the way you communicate means rewiring your brain.**

- **Repetition is the key to ingraining a new habit.**

- **The best approach is to work on one skill at a time.**

- **In spite of your best intentions, at first your old habits will kick in.**

- **Reflect on your shortfalls, learn from them, and rededicate yourself.**

- **If you consistently make the effort to apply what you've learned and if you persist through frustration, the new skill will eventually become your habitual way of communicating.**

- **It helps to have a coach to hold you accountable and offer encouragement.**

Learn more about skill-building:

- Josh Kaufman, *The First 20 Hours* (Penguin, 2013)
- Charles Duhigg, *The Power of Habit* (Random House, 2012)

....

The Top 10 Parent-Child Communication Skills

I've been helping adults learn interpersonal skills for decades, and I'm aware that there are dozens of such skills. The 10 skills that are the focus of this book have the greatest potential to help you pass on wisdom and life skills to your young adult-in-progress.

The purpose of this section is to coach you to acquire the skills that resolve issues and foster optimum child development while nurturing the bond with your child:

- Listen to understand

- Coach your child to think

- Guide learning from experience

- Get buy-in for expectations

- Offer encouragement

- Express appreciation

- Give feedback constructively

- Accept feedback graciously

- Engage in dialogue
- Resolve conflict creatively

"Most people do not listen with the intent to understand; they listen with the intent to speak."

Stephen Covey

"You can see a lot, just by listening."

Yogi Berra

4

....

Listen to Understand

The heart of the skill described in this chapter was first called "active listening" by Thomas Gordon, who made it the center-piece of his 1970 book, *P.E.T – Parent Effectiveness Training*. This way of listening, adapted from techniques used by thera-pists and counselors, has also been referred to as "reflective lis-tening" and "empathic listening." I prefer Stephen Covey's term: "listening to understand."

Listening to understand is the most important aspect of effective parent-child communication.

Whatever the reason for your interaction, you won't be do-ing all the talking. Your child will have something to say, and you'll need to hear it and understand it. This is why I encourage you to work on listening skills first; and I recommend you get comfortable with listening before you work on any of the other communication skills.

Your child won't make it easy for you to listen well. For one thing, they're on the front end of a slow process of experiment-ing with new opinions, preferences and identities. So they may be unsure of themselves; and as they deal with their mistakes, problems and disappointments, they tend to keep their thoughts and feelings to themselves.

Also, when they do open up, it's almost never in the form of a logical, well-organized speech. The points they're trying to make, which they may not fully grasp themselves, could be heavily laced with emotion and mixed with stories, opinions, complaints, demands, and feelings—in no particular order. They might start with whatever is on their mind and go from there. Along the way, they might digress. In other words, the meaning could be hard to sort out.

If you aren't a skilled listener—and most parents aren't—you're likely to do more talking than listening, reacting with your own feelings, seeing the situation from your adult point of view, and misinterpreting your child's message. If your teen feels that you don't understand, they may conclude you don't care about what they're trying to say and that it's too hard to get through to you.

The consequences of a failure to communicate can be huge. For one thing, you'll miss a precious opportunity to sense who your kid is becoming and what they're going through at this time of their life. Your child might feel disrespected and misunderstood and wonder if coming to you with their issues is worth the effort. In other words, the bond you had with your child in the early years might begin to come apart at the seams. Poor listening—not hormones—is the main reason young people distance themselves from their parents.

Consider this situation, where a daughter has just handed her father her report card:

Dad: "I see you got a C in English."

Daughter: "Yeah, well..."

Dad: "This is unacceptable." (JUDGING)

Daughter: "I hate English."

Dad: "But you used to love it. You used to get A's." (LOGIC)

Daughter: "Mr. Brown is a dork."

Dad: "A dork?" (SARCASM)

Daughter: "All he does is read from the book we've already read. And then he tells us stuff about his personal life. It's a waste of time. I'm not learning anything. I hate it."

Dad: "Your grades are important. You have to do the work anyway, no matter who your teacher is." (PREACHING)

Daughter: "I can't listen to him. I check out and think about other stuff."

Dad: "Well, you've got to deal with it. No more C's. I want to see an A next time. No excuses." (ULTIMATUM)

Dad isn't being a jerk. Clearly, he cares about his daughter's future and has high expectations. The conversation is a fairly typical one, though; the way he responds to her complaint is unsympathetic. Whatever she's trying to say isn't getting through, and the real issue isn't being addressed or resolved. In a sense, he brushes her off. The daughter will be understandably unhappy with the exchange.

It's easy to forget that growing up is a difficult journey, that gaining life wisdom and life skills takes years—if it happens at all. What's needed at this time of life is an attitude of empathy and openness. Otherwise, kids will stop trying to share what's going on in their lives.

Even people who've had training in how to listen and tried to practice the skills in their lives discover how hard it is to simply recognize when they should be using the skill. That's when old habits kick in. Instead of listening for the meaning and checking for understanding, they engage in conversation, offer their own opinions and stories, and explain what their child should be doing. These failures are discouraging to both parent and child.

A colleague of mine, who happens to be an experienced trainer of listening skills, told me about an incident that happened to her several years ago when her daughter was in high school. Her daughter had experienced a difficult situation with one of the children she'd been babysitting, and she was upset when she got home. As my friend listened to her describe what happened, she reacted as a caring mother, jumping into problem-solving mode, asking a lot of questions and then offering suggestions about how her daughter could have handled the situation differently. As her daughter continued to talk about her frustrations, Mom continued to offer advice.

Finally, the girl said emphatically, *"Mom, I don't need your suggestions. I had a horrible day. All I really wanted you to do is listen and be sympathetic. I've already taken care of this."* These words stopped the mother in her tracks. She realized her daughter was looking for understanding and compassion, not criticism or advice.

All these years later, my colleague still remembers how easy it was to disregard her own guidance about best listening practices. That's why I emphasize that mastering listening and the other skills is a *lifetime* pursuit.

Listening moments and the listening mindset

The first step to listening well is being on the lookout for opportunities to listen—what I call "listening moments"—when your child wants to tell you something. These occasions might include behaviors that take you by surprise: emotional outbursts, unexpected problems, mistakes in judgment, bad attitudes, or a point of view contrary to your own. Naturally you'll feel your own emotional response: disappointment, frustration, or anger. These feelings are your signal that *this is a listening moment*, not an occasion to react. Once you realize you need to be listening, the next step is to check that you're in the proper frame of mind for listening—what I call the "listening mindset."

Recognize the "listening moment"

...when your child is trying to tell you something you need to hear.

Engage your "listening mindset"

I care about my child's problems, thoughts, and feelings. Something is going on with them right now, and I want to know what it is. So rather than react negatively or assume I understand, I check what I'm hearing.

Thinking these thoughts at the right time will be like using the power of love to turn on your parent-child radar and set it at the right listening frequency. They set you up for listening to understand, which involves four skills:

1. **Give your child your undivided attention.**

2. **Sense what they're feeling and express empathy.**

3. **Listen for the meaning and check what you think you understand.**

4. **Encourage your child to continue talking until you're sure you understand what they're trying to say.**

Listening skill 1: Give your child your undivided attention.

In his book, *What Got You Here Won't Get You There*, executive coach Marshall Goldsmith says that former president Bill Clinton was an "absolute master" at giving his attention to anyone who spoke to him. "He acted as if you were the only person in the room. Every fiber of his being, from his eyes to his body language, communicated that he was locked into what you were saying. He conveyed how important you were, not how important he was."

Whether your child is venting or you sense something is bothering them, this is a precious opportunity to prove you care about what they're trying to say, that they can get through to you. Once you realize that this is a listening moment and your mind is set for listening, make finding out what's going on in your child's head your top priority. Stop what you're doing and do what Bill Clinton is said to have done: *consciously focus 100% on your child.*

Multi-tasking or fiddling with objects will distract your attention. Stop what you're doing, put down your phone, book, or pen, and turn to face your child. Try to keep your mind clear, because even your thoughts, feelings, opinions, memories, and imagination can distract you from hearing what your child is saying. If necessary, take your child to another room or outside where you can face each other in relative quiet and privacy. Communicate through your posture and facial expressions that *your child is the most important person in your world right now.* From time to time, give them an accepting smile, a nod, or an occasional "uh-huh" or "I see" to indicate that you're focused and listening.

Listening skill 2: Sense what they're feeling and express empathy.

Most of the time, what you sense will be a combination of thoughts and emotions. Sometimes your child will lead with what they're feeling. Many of the opportunities to connect with your child will be triggered by emotions such as joy or frustration. Other times they'll be able to speak in a rational way about their issue. Even then, you may pick up on how they feel about it. No one knows your child as intimately as you do, and showing you understand their needs and feelings will make it easier for them to open up.

Mindfulness is a crucial first step to expressing empathy. Mindfulness means focusing on the present moment to be fully aware of what's in front of you. No one is in this state of mind all the time. In a busy day, most parents only intermittently experience moments of intense mindfulness. You may be aware of your child, but in a kind of distant way. You may be focused on other things, your own problems and feelings. This is normal.

Before expressing empathy, you need to experience it. And to experience empathy, you need to be mindful of your child, sensing what they're experiencing and feeling. You need to shift from your own thoughts and feelings to sensing your child in the here-and-now. Your parental love is most real and intense when you're able to experience your child without the filter of whatever may be going on in your mind: without judging, reacting, thinking about something that happened, or paying attention to your own thoughts and feelings. Only when you're mindfully aware of your child is an empathic connection possible.

Mark Goulston, in his book, *Just Listen*, says this about empathy:

> *"Making someone 'feel felt' simply means putting yourself in the other person's shoes. When you succeed, you can change the dynamics of a relationship in a heartbeat. At that instant, instead of trying to get the better of each other, you 'get' each other and the breakthrough can lead to cooperation, collaboration, and effective communication."*

In my experience, expressing empathy follows three steps:

1. **Be "in the moment" with your child.** Empty your mind of every thought and feeling about what may have happened. Consciously focus on who this young person

is, right now. Observe facial expressions, posture, gestures, and tone of voice.

2. **Imagine what your child is feeling.** Put yourself in your child's situation—not to agree or disagree, and not to judge, but simply to be aware of and understand your child's experience.

3. **Three ways to express what your child is feeling:**

   - *Ask:* "Are you disappointed that Dad couldn't watch you play?"

   - *Assume:* "You must be disappointed that Dad couldn't show up for the game. You wanted him to see you out there hustling."

   - *Express the feeling:* "It's disappointing when you want Dad to see you at your best, and he can't be there."

Listening skill 3: Listen for the meaning and check what you think you understand.

The biggest mistake parents make when listening is assuming they understand what their kid is trying to say. The truth is, even skilled communicators sometimes miss the point. So with your attention focused on what your child is saying, listen for the meaning. Interpret both the verbal and nonverbal messages, and ask yourself: *Why is my child telling me this?* And when you think you understand some of what your child is expressing, check to be sure. The skill: *In your own words, tell your child what you think you've understood so far.*

"Are you saying that...?"

"Do you mean that...?"

"It sounds like...."

"So what you're getting at is...."

"Let me see if I heard you right. You...."

The skill is *not* to repeat verbatim what you child has said. Instead, express what you think they're getting at—the *meaning* of what they've said. Don't worry that you'll get it wrong. The important thing is to *check your understanding*. If your interpretation misses the point, your kid will let you know; you'll sense their frustration. They may even correct you. As they try to explain, continue listening for the meaning and once again check what you think you understand.

Listening skill 4. Encourage your child to continue talking until you're sure you understand what they're trying to say.

Most of the time you won't hear the whole story all at once. Even if your child verifies that you've correctly understood what you've heard so far, they may not have gotten to the point. They probably have more to say. You may have to check your understanding several times before getting to the core of the issue.

So ask another open-ended question to encourage your child to continue talking—not so you can offer your opinion or advice, but to be sure you hear the whole story. Remember, an open-ended question is the kind of question that gets the speaker to say what's on their mind. It doesn't ask for specific information, which can be given in a one- or two-word answer, such as "No," or "Twice," or "Mr. Howard." Replies to factual questions tend to halt an interchange rather than keep it going. Here are some examples of how to encourage your child to continue:

"Go on."

"And then what happened?"

"Why do you think he did that?"

"What was the real issue?"

"What are some other ways you could have handled the situation?"

"Which approach will work best for you?"

"How will this affect your decision?"

"What's your plan?"

Sometimes you can tell your child is having a bad day but isn't saying anything. Showing that you've noticed can get them to open up. This may create a listening moment.

Dad: "What's going on, son?"

Son: "Nothing."

Dad: "You don't seem like your usual self. Is something bothering you?" (CHECKING NONVERBAL MESSAGE)

Son: "No, not really."

Dad: "Okay, you know you can talk to me about anything, anytime."

Son: "It's just some stupid thing. I saw Craig take my pen from my backpack and when I said I wanted it back he said he didn't take it."

Dad: "Why do you think he lied?" (OPEN-ENDED QUESTION)

Son: "I have no idea."

Dad: "What's your best guess?"

Son: "Maybe he needed a pen. Maybe he was embarrassed that he got caught."

Dad: "So you're a little bummed about it." (CHECKING MESSAGE)

Son: "Yeah, I guess so."

Dad: "What do you plan to do about it?"

Son: "Nothing. It's just a cheap pen."

Dad: "But Craig's your friend, isn't he?"

Son: "Not really, I guess not."

Dad: "I see. Because he took your pen?" (CHECKING MESSAGE)

Son: "And lied about it. I'm not sure I trust him anymore. I have other friends."

Whenever you encourage your child to think through their problems (without offering your own solutions), you're helping them exercise critical thinking. The magical thing about this way of listening is that your child verifies your interpretation, so *you know they feel they've been heard and understood*, which inspires a feeling of connectedness that reinforces the bond between you.

Listening this way often has a wonderful bonus: it can clarify your child's thinking *for your child*. When they open up to you, at first they may be distressed, but they may not know exactly what's bothering them. They may be anxious or upset and not know why. When you achieve an understanding of the underlying issue, this could be a useful revelation for them, too—satisfying outcomes for both of you.

If you're like most parents, listening to understand will mean replacing old communication habits with new ones. This means time, effort and persistence, because your old habits are physically wired circuits in your brain. Once again, if you sometimes forget to listen to understand, or if your efforts seem awkward, this is a normal aspect of the skill-building process. As I emphasized in Chapter 3 ("The Secret to Improving Communication Skills"), *the key is to keep trying*. If you stick with it, using the skill will begin to feel easier and more natural.

Let's revisit that unpleasant "C"...

Dad: "I see you got a C in English."

Daughter: "Yeah, well..."

Dad: "Why do you think you didn't get your usual A?" (OPEN-ENDED QUESTION)

Daughter: "I hate English."

Dad: "You're not happy with your English course." (CHECKING MEANING)

Daughter: "Not the course so much as the teacher, Mr. Brown. He just reads from the text and tells stories about his personal life. I've already read the book, so I'm not learning anything."

Dad: "You don't like the way he teaches." (CHECKING MEANING)

Daughter: "He's smart and entertaining, but he's wasting my time rather than helping me learn. That's what's so upsetting."

Dad: "So he has something to offer, but he's not giving it to you." (CHECKING MEANING)

Daughter: "Yes! I want to learn to write better, and I love literature, but he's not helping us with any of that."

Dad: "You feel he should take a different approach." (CHECKING MEANING)

Daughter: "I wish he would, but I don't know what to do about it."

Dad: "Do you have any ideas?" (LETTING CHILD OWN THE PROBLEM)

Daughter: "What can I do? I'm just a student. He's the teacher."

Dad: "You don't think you can change the way he teaches." (CHECKING MEANING)

Daughter: "I should be making an A, but I'm totally turned off. I ought to give him a piece of my mind."

Dad: "How do you feel about doing that?" (OPEN-ENDED QUESTION)

Daughter: "I wouldn't know what to say."

Dad: "You're not sure how to express your frustration." (CHECKING MEANING)

Daughter: "Maybe I should just tell him. What have I got to lose? The class couldn't be much worse."

Dad: "You think being honest with him might work." (CHECKING MEANING)

Daughter: "Maybe. Especially if I don't get in his face. Just tell him what I need in the class. Tell him I enjoy English and want to learn."

Dad: "How do you think he'll respond to that?" (OPEN-ENDED QUESTION)

Daughter: "I don't know. It might work. He's actually a nice guy."

Dad: "Sounds like you have a plan." (CHECKING MEANING)

Daughter: "I'll give it a try. What's he going to do? Give me an F?"

You may have to work to understand what your child is trying to say. But it's worth it. At no point did Dad get critical or aggressive or try to tell his daughter how to handle her situation. Instead, he encouraged her to think it through herself, and she came up with a solution she's willing to try. Instead of feeling like a failure, she feels she has a chance to deal with her problem.

Tips for optimum listening:

- **Watch out for emotional reactions.** Old habits die hard, and when your child annoys or upsets you, you may catch yourself reacting emotionally or falling back on authority. The feeling of rising emotions is usually a signal to listen instead.

- **Review your "Listening Mindset."** You may have trouble engaging the right mindset for listening if you're not clear about what it is.

- **Be careful not to engage in conversation when you need to be listening.** Think of conversation and listening as two different things. Conversation involves sharing each other's stories, opinions, etc. It's a great way to nurture a connection with someone. There's a time to enjoy conversation and a time to focus on listening. Sometimes when you're just talking, you'll sense that your child wants to tell you something. If you understand the difference between conversation and listening, you can consciously shift into a listening mode.

- **Don't interrupt.** Listening is about the other person, not you. Interrupting your child with your own input will frustrate them because it makes it hard for them to complete their thought. Also, it implies that what you have to say is more important than what your child has to say. Remember: your job is to understand, so your child should be doing most of the talking.

- **Be flexible about how you use the four listening skills.** One good approach is to use the skills in the sequence described above. However, after you've become aware of a listening moment and have engaged your listening mindset, sometimes performing any one of the four steps in isolation can be effective. For example, expressing empathy is a powerful way of connecting and in certain situations can, by itself, achieve the understanding you seek. The same is true of listening for the meaning and checking the message. If the issue your child is struggling with is not an emotional one, expressing empathy may not be needed. And if you're lucky, the message will be a straightforward one, and your child can get to the point without further discussion. Even if you skip the empathy step, you can use it later in your listening if you sense that the emotional element is more of a factor than you initially thought. At other times, simply encouraging them to continue speaking can be enough for them to clarify their thinking and even achieve a resolution.

- **Don't offer your experience, advice or solutions.** Once you understand your child's issue, it's a mistake to feel responsible for resolving it. Yes, you have more life experience and wisdom. But at this stage of life, they're capable of figuring out how to deal with their issues, and doing so will help them gain skills they'll need as an adult. You may sense that the solution they come up with has little chance of working, and you'll want to suggest a better approach. Giving advice and suggesting solutions will block your child from thinking creatively about options. Unless their solution puts them in danger, give your child the opportunity to take responsibility for their life and learn from mistakes. Ask open-ended questions that get them to think about the root of the problem, possible solutions, their ultimate decision, and their action steps.

- **Keep an open mind. Don't disagree, take offense or argue.** You may hear opinions or ideas that surprise you. Rather than reacting negatively, which would block communication, consider this an opportunity to combine listening with dialogue (more on this in Chapter 12, "Engage in Dialogue"). For example: If a young person offers an idea that bothers you, instead of rejecting or criticizing it, respond with listening to make sure you understand what your child is suggesting. Then do three things: (1) state what you like about the idea (there are no perfectly good or perfectly bad ideas!); (2) explain your concerns; and (3) ask if your child is interested in exploring ways to improve the idea to address the concerns.

- **When listening to your child, be patient.** It may be as hard for your child to explain what's on their mind as it is for you to grasp the explanation. It's a rare child—or adult, for that matter—who gets straight to the point. When listening, it can help to ask yourself, *Why is my child telling me this?*

Golden opportunities to exercise listening with your child:

- Your child comes to you wanting to talk
- When you try using one of the listening subskills and your child responds
- You and your child disagree
- Your child makes a case for something they want
- You give feedback and your child gets defensive
- You notice a change in mood, either positive or negative

- After asking an open-ended question, listen to understand the answer

To get your "reps," stay alert for listening moments like these:

- **Practice listening with other adults.** Listening to understand is an adult-to-adult human relationship skill that works no matter who you use it with. So in addition to using it with your child, practice listening to understand with friends, family, and coworkers. The more you exercise listening to understand, the quicker your brain will rewire itself.

- **Look for listening moments when using other skills.** In the chapters ahead, you'll learn that listening is a key element of other communication skills: coaching your child to think, giving feedback, offering encouragement, engaging in dialogue, and resolving conflict. Each of these skills can stimulate your child to talk, so each of them will produce a special "listening moment."

- **Remember that becoming a more effective listener is a journey.** While this approach to listening to understand makes sense, you'll need to practice to get comfortable with it. The first few times you try the skill, it won't feel natural. But keep at it. The more experience you gain, the more your confidence will build. The key is not to expect a 100% success rate at first. Give yourself credit for your successful efforts—good advice for learning any skill. The more you apply the skill, the easier it will get and the more often you'll experience success. No matter how many times you miss an opportunity to listen or forget to use one of the steps, recognize what happened and remind yourself to apply the skill next time. You can always revisit this chapter to remind yourself of what to do. With experience, you'll be the kind of listener your child needs you to be.

- **Keep the goal in mind.** Listening to understand is one of those skills, like chess or tennis, that you can continue to improve indefinitely. And the better you get, the more your adolescent child will open up to you, because they'll feel they've been heard, respected and understood. Your child's self-esteem and the bond between you will grow stronger.

This chapter in a nutshell:

- **Listening effectively is a vital component of many other communication skills.**

- **Listening well is how you find out what's happening with your child. Also, it causes them to feel understood and appreciated, which promotes a strong relationship.**

- **Effective listening begins with giving your undivided attention.**

- **You need to recognize when you need to listen— listening moments—and engage the right attitude—the listening mindset.**

- **When you express empathy, you learn what your child is feeling.**

- **When you check for understanding, you learn what your child is trying to say.**

- **It may take a while to hear the whole message, so encourage your child to continue.**

Learn more about listening:

- Mark Goulston, *Just Listen* (Amacom, 2015)
- Thomas Gordon, *Parent Effectiveness Training* (Three Rivers, 2000)
- Stephen R. Covey, *The 7 Habits of Highly Effective Families* (Golden, 1997)
- Susan Stiffelman, *Parenting with Presence* (New World, 2015)

"Children must be taught how to think, not what to think."

Margaret Mead

"Education is not the learning of facts, but the training of the mind to think."

Albert Einstein

"It is not what you do for your children, but what you have taught them to do for themselves, that will make them successful."

Ann Landers

5

....

Coach Your Child to Think

Imagine that your child is now an adult, working at a new job and building a life. You know that most of what matters is going to be hard:

- Finding a fulfilling role

- Building rapport with managers and coworkers

- Creating lasting personal relationships

- Managing finances

- Owning and maintaining a home

- Raising a family

- Learning new life skills

- Solving problems that come up every day

- Dealing with tragedy

Some young adults struggle with relatively easy tasks, such as making dinner or doing laundry. So someday when your grown child runs up against the inevitable frustrations and challenges, which would you prefer they do:

A. Call and ask for help

B. Handle it without your help

If you're missing your child, you might be delighted to have the call, whether the news is good or bad. You have tons of life experience, and you may feel that sharing your wisdom or advice is an expression of parental love. If so, you might be tempted to choose A.

But the better answer is B. Assuming your own parents are still alive, do you lean on them for solutions whenever you have a crisis? Very likely you just confront the problem, think it through, decide what you want to do, and then do it. And if it doesn't turn out the way you planned, you learn from your effort and try something else. Because that's what adults do.

The best-case scenario is that your child becomes an independent adult, confident that they can deal with whatever comes up next. But this capacity doesn't suddenly turn on just because they're fully grown and gone. The ability to create a life in today's world requires core strengths, life skills, and a variety of creative and critical thinking skills. The ideal way to acquire these essential adult skills is to exercise them repeatedly during the years before they leave home.

Recognize that your child is an adult-in-the-making and that you have a limited amount of time to help them prepare. Rather than shielding your child from challenges and frustrations, help them get used to resolving issues on their own. As they try to think for themselves, you can be there with empathy, support, and encouragement. The basic approach is simple:

Ask open-ended questions that get your child to think.

An open-ended question is one that can't be answered with a simple "yes" or "no" or a word or two. This fairly simple communication technique is the opposite of using your superior knowledge, skills and experience to give answers and advice. While doing the thinking for them may resolve the immediate issue, it won't help your child create the brain circuits for thinking.

The first step is noticing opportunities to stimulate thinking:

Recognize the "thinking moment"

...when you can encourage your child to do their own thinking, rather than give them the answer or solution.

Engage your "thinking mindset"

I ask open-ended questions that encourage my child to practice thinking: understanding, reasoning, evaluating, problem-solving, decision-making, goal-setting, planning, and organizing.

Open-ended questions can take many forms, depending on the situation. Here are nine typical opportunities for helping your child wire their brain for patterns of good judgment and decision-making, along with examples of open-ended questions.

When your child doesn't UNDERSTAND HOW OR WHY

Things happen for a reason. Young people may be aware of what's going on around them, but they may not ask themselves why. If they aren't coached to be curious during adolescence, this habit of mind may never get wired, and they may not become inquisitive adults.

A parent can encourage a child to ponder how things relate to each other or to understand the connection between cause and effect. The key is to get your child to notice ordinary things and ask "why."

For example, say you and your child are getting in the car to run an errand. If they complain about having to fasten the seatbelt, you could ask: "Why do you think the state made it a law?" Or if you notice that people are getting their gas tanks filled at a station when gas is cheaper only two blocks down the street, you could point this out and ask: "Why do you think they're doing that?

Some possible questions:

"What do these things have in common?"

"In what way is [A] different from [B]?"

"Why do you think [A] is more interesting than [B]?"

"Why is this important to you?"

"Why do you think this situation exists?"

"What does this mean?"

"How does this work?"

"Why do you think this happened?"

"Why do you think she said that?"

"What was the artist trying to express?"

"Why do you think I want you to do this?"

The idea is to encourage your child to think about why the world works the way it does.

At breakfast, a mother is reading the lifestyle section of the newspaper. She initiates conversation by asking her daughter an open-ended question:

Mom: "Have you noticed how fashions change every year? If a style is so appealing, why do you suppose designers always change them?"

Daughter: "To get people to keep spending money on clothes?"

Mom: "That makes sense. How do you feel about that?"

Dad and son are playing catch with a football. During a break, Dad asks:

Dad: "Hey, can you feel how your cheek that faces the sun is warm, and the other side feels cooler?"

Son: "Yeah."

Dad: "It's pretty hot out here. Why do you think one cheek feels cooler?"

Son: "I guess because the sun is hot and one cheek is facing the sun and the other isn't."

Dad: "Right. But the sun is a long way from here. How is it that the sun is so far away but can still make your skin feel warm?"

You may be asking your child to do a kind of thinking they're not used to, so don't be surprised if you sometimes get the answer, "I don't know." This is an honest answer, but a lazy one. The key is to not give your own explanation. Instead, encourage your child to think it through or search for an answer. Say something like, "Yeah, it's not so obvious. But think about it. I'd like to know what you think."

When you want your child to FOCUS ON THE FUTURE

Most of the time, kids are focused on the present, only rarely pondering the future.

You may want your child to learn the kind of life skills they'll need as adults, but they won't be motivated to do this if they can't imagine a future when these skills will become necessary. To take schoolwork seriously, they have to understand how it might help them later when they're on their own. To avoid a dreadful consequence, they need to imagine what might happen. You want your child to save their money, but they'll be motivated to do this only if they've thought about the future reward for doing so. To set a goal, a child has to have something worth working towards—something they can achieve in the future. Many of your efforts to parent will stall if the future doesn't seem real to them.

To get your child used to imagining the future, try asking questions like these:

"What are you planning to do this weekend?"

"How do you want to spend the summer when the school year is over?"

"What plans do you have for the money you're earning?"

"How do you see yourself using the car once you get a license?"

"What do you hope to do after you graduate from high school?"

When you want your child to FORESEE CONSEQUENCES

One aspect of focusing on the future is knowing that a specific action causes a certain result. This requires imagining something that hasn't happened yet. If a child has observed cause and effect in the past, they can apply the memory of this connection to a similar situation in the future.

For example, say your child wants to go white-water rafting with friends instead of spending two weeks visiting relatives.

"How do you think your relatives will feel if we show up without you?"

"What do you think could happen on this kind of adventure?"

"What skills will you need to do it safely?"

The idea is to get your child to think about what causes things to happen and to imagine what might happen as a result of their actions. This mental skill is vital to impulse control, good judgment and decision-making.

Typical questions:

"In this situation, what do you think will happen?"

"What do you hope to get out of this?"

"How will this help you achieve your goal?"

"If you do this, what could happen next?"

"What other ways can you get what you want?"

"What could get in your way?"

"Why doesn't this feel right to you?"

"Based on what you know about her, what do you think she'll say?"

"What bad things might happen if you do what you're thinking about doing?"

The key is to avoid doing the thinking for your child, which is what you may have had to do when they were younger.

When your child needs to SET GOALS AND MAKE PLANS

Your child may decide to try out for the track team next year. Or they may want to earn enough money to buy the latest smartphone. To get there from here will involve a number of steps. If they have a plan and follow it, they're not only more likely to succeed, but their self-esteem will grow if they do. Once your child is comfortable thinking about future goals, they can envision how to make it happen.

Typical questions:

"What would you like to achieve this year?"

"What will you need to do to get that?"

"What's most important to you?"

"What's your No. 1 goal right now?"

"What do you want to do after graduation?"

"What are your other options?"

"How much will this cost you?"

"What are the advantages and disadvantages of your plan?"

"How will doing this benefit you?"

"What will you need to do to get that?"

"What would be your best first step?"

"What's the hardest challenge you'll have to face?"

"If this happens, how will you deal with it?"

"What help or resources will you need?"

"If you go with this plan, how do you think it will work out?"

To see a clearer path to achieving a goal, your child could write down the action steps. If they write each necessary action on a post-it note, later they can easily rearrange them in time or cause-and-effect sequence. Listen to clarify what your child says, while avoiding lecturing, explaining, or trying to solve their problem. In other words, ask questions to get your child to do the planning.

One good way to teach planning skills is to involve your child in preparing for family events.

Mom: "Are you looking forward to our trip to the mountains?"

Son: "Definitely."

Mom: "I'm going to need your help."

Son: "What do you mean?"

Mom: You know how busy I am at work right now. I'd like you to figure out what we're going to need for the trip—from start to finish. We leave a week from Friday. I need you to pull it all together so we're ready to go. Can you do that?"

Son: "Sure."

A few days later, the son asks, "Do you think I should fill the gas tank?"

Mom: "What do you think?"

Son: "I guess so. And what about food? What do you want me to pack?"

Mom: "Well there's four of us and we don't come back until Monday night. Figure it out and make sure we have enough."

When you want your child to EVALUATE something

One aspect of good judgment is the ability to appreciate the better option—the ability to assess the value of something. You can help your child become a more discerning thinker by asking questions like:

"How are these three options different?"

"What does this do for you?"

"Why is this better than that?"

"What are the advantages of doing this?"

"What are the downsides?"

"What do you like most about that?"

"What do you admire about this?"

"What are its best features?"

"What's wrong with it?"

"How well does it do what it's supposed to do?"

"Why do you think this is worth the price?"

"How safe is this?"

"How is this good for you?"

"What are the strengths of that argument?"

"Why is that movie one of your favorites?"

"What message do you think the artist is expressing?"

"How well does that person do this?"

"What do you think about how well this is made?"

When you want your child to BE MORE SELF-AWARE

As young people begin to seek independence, they want to fit in with their peer groups. They'll be concerned about how others see them. But there's a big difference between conforming and becoming an individual. As they seek an identity, they might experiment with roles and looks, or they might begin the serious work of creating who they want to be. Parents can help by asking questions that encourage self-awareness:

"What's your opinion about that?"

"When something like this happens, how do you feel?"

"What makes you feel happy?"

"What makes you angry?"

"What do you feel you're good at?"

"In what areas would you like to improve?"

"How do you think others see you?"

"What about yourself would you like to improve?"

"What's most important to you?"

"What do you look forward to most these days?"

When you want your child to STAY FOCUSED

Because the prefrontal cortex (PFC) is heavily interconnected with other parts of the brain, it receives real-time input and can stimulate other areas of the brain. For example, when we dream, remember or imagine, the PFC sends signals to the visual cortex to create images. The amygdala is an inner part of your brain that sends fight-or-flight alarm signals. The PFC, which is connected to it, can quickly evaluate this input and decide whether to send a signal back to calm the amygdala. If the senses notice something, such as an unusual noise or smell, the PFC can evaluate how important the information is, and then direct the brain to focus on it or pay attention to something else. In this way, it's possible to learn how to manage attention, ignore distractions, and stay focused. These questions can help a child wire their PFC for the skills of staying focused:

"What you're doing right now—how important is it to you?"

"During the next hour, what do you want to accomplish?"

"What can you do next to get back on track?"

"What should you be paying attention to right now?"

"What's the payoff for finishing this?"

"What can you postpone until later?"

"When somebody wants you to do something, what's a nice way to say no thanks?"

Guide your child to THINK THROUGH PROBLEMS AND CHALLENGES

Say your child is upset because they forgot they promised to help a friend work on a project, but then arranged to meet someone else at the same time. Or they want to buy an expensive item and don't have the money to pay for it. Or they put off writing an essay that's due the next day.

Typical questions:

"What's causing this problem?"

"What do you think went wrong?"

"How have you dealt with situations like this in the past?"

"What options do you have?"

"What's possible in this situation?"

"Which is more important to you, [A] or [B]?"

"Is there an even better way to…?"

"Why do you feel this option is the best one?"

"If you do that, how will it meet your needs?"

"How will doing this benefit the other people involved?"

"Is there an option that will be acceptable to everyone?"

"What are the potential dangers?"

"What could this end up costing you?"

"What does your gut tell you?"

"To get started, what should you do first?"

The idea is to ask questions that lead your child to go through the typical steps of problem-solving: identifying the real problem, thinking of possible solutions, considering the pros and cons of each option, picking the best one, and making a plan. Even though you want the best for your child and have lots of experience, keep in mind that it's your child's problem, not yours. Recognize the opportunity for them to exercise problem-solving skills, and resist the temptation to push your idea of the best solution.

Dad: "You seem down today."

Daughter: "I didn't get the lab assistant job."

Dad: "I'm sorry, Kiddo. I know you prepared for it."

Daughter: "They picked my friend Ella."

Dad: "How do you feel about that?"

Daughter: "Well it's nice for her. But I was counting on the money. I was going to use it to pay for the Paris trip. Now I don't know what to do."

Dad: "I know you had your heart set on it. What other options do you have to get the money?"

Daughter: "I don't know. None."

Dad: "What can you do to find out?"

Daughter: "I guess I could check the want ads. Or I could just go to the mall. Maybe some of the stores still have 'We're Hiring' signs in the window."

Dad: "Does that sound promising?"

Daughter: "I think I'll go down there. I remember seeing signs at some of the clothing stores. I might get lucky."

Dad: "Sounds like it's worth a try. Do you have other options?"

Daughter: "Well, the lab assistant job is gone. But maybe the school has some other jobs open. I could check."

Dad: "So you're going to check both?"

Daughter: "Yeah. And while I'm at it, I'll talk to Mrs. Bath, the guidance counselor. She's kind of plugged in."

Dad: "Go for it, Kiddo."

When you want your child to SELF-REGULATE AND CONTROL IMPULSES

When kids get angry, they might express rage by striking out or saying something hurtful. While this is a common behavior for small children, it can be disastrous for teens or adults to act this way. It's possible for young people to learn to be aware of their emotions, consciously pause until the emotions subside, and consider more effective responses. Here are some questions that can help your child learn to stay cool in heated situations:

"What are you feeling right now?"

"Why do you feel this way?"

"What do you feel like doing?"

"If you do that, what could happen?"

"What would happen if you wait to say or do something?"

"What can you do to calm yourself?"

"Why do you think this person did this?"

"What can you say or do that will benefit you the most?"

All the questions suggested in this chapter are variations of *What do you think?* When there's an opportunity to ponder, discover, think ahead, learn, plan, or deal with problems, open-ended questions can coach your child to think for themselves. Each time you ask for your child's thoughts, you'll send the message that you value what they have to say, which will build their self-esteem.

To get your "reps," stay alert for thinking moments like these:

- You sense a potential problem situation, but your child doesn't appreciate the consequences

- Your child has a problem

- Your child is facing a difficult decision

- Your child is wasting time or losing focus

- Your child has made a mistake

- After experiencing disappointment or failure, your child is upset

This chapter in a nutshell:

- **To possess critical thinking skills as an adult, your child will need to create habits for them now.**

- **There are lots of ways to encourage your child to improve their thinking.**

- **The key is asking open-ended questions—countless variations of *What do you think?***

Learn more about encouraging your child to think for themselves:

- David Rock, *Quiet Leadership* (Harper Business, 2007)

- Jane Healy, *How to Have Intelligent and Creative Conversations with Your Kids* (Doubleday, 1992)

- Dennis Coates, *How Your Teen Can Grow a Smarter Brain*, 2nd Ed. (First Summit, 2020)

"There are no mistakes or failures, only lessons."

Denis Waitley

6

....

Guide Learning from Experience

The previous chapter introduced you to several ways to help your child get in the habit of doing their own thinking. One of the most valuable opportunities for getting your child to think is to encourage them to learn from the good things and the bad things that happen to them.

It's often said that experience is the best teacher and that the value of mistakes is the lessons you learn from them. There's a lot of wisdom in this. But to capture the lesson, a child needs to think about what happened and why. Young people sometimes experience success; but they don't always think about what worked so they can repeat the success in the future.

And when they fall short, they don't always ponder why. Learning from mistakes doesn't happen automatically. In a busy day it's all too easy to go from situation to situation without giving much thought to what happened. But if not much is learned, a child is more likely to repeat mistakes.

Consciously learning from experience not only helps them stay on track and do what works, it actually accelerates their development. These are compelling reasons to make a habit of reflecting on why things happen the way they do. As a concerned parent, you can encourage your child to do this.

The key is to get good at spotting a "learning moment"—when something significant has happened to your child, whether it's a success or a failure. When you sense excitement, agitation, anger or depression, this is your hint to take a few moments to ask the questions that will help them discover the lesson.

Recognize the "learning moment"

...when something significant has happened, and your child can learn from it.

Engage your "learning mindset"

I ask open-ended questions that encourage my child to analyze what happened so they can improve the way they approach problems in the future.

You encourage this kind of learning by asking these open-ended questions:

1. **What happened?** The details of an event need to be recalled in order to make sense of them. What was the sequence of events? What did you do? How did others react? How do you feel about it?

2. **Why did you handle it this way?** Things happen for a reason. To imagine a better way to handle a situation like this, try to understand why things occurred the way they did. What were you thinking? What helped or hindered? What led to the outcome?

3. **What were the consequences?** Appreciating the impact of what happened creates the motivation to handle situations like this more effectively. Benefits? Costs? Problems? Resolutions?

4. **How would you handle a similar situation in the future?** What did you learn from this experience? What basic principles? How are you going to apply the lesson?

5. **What are your next steps?** What will you do in the next day or two to set you up for implementing this learning?

When you ask one of the questions, listen to understand what your child is telling you.

Dad: "What's wrong?"

Son: "Nothing."

Dad: "You slammed the front door just now."

Son: "So I'm sorry already!"

Dad: "You seem upset about something."

Son: "No I'm not."

Dad: "Tell me what happened."

Son: "It's no big deal. Just Jerry being a jerk."

Dad: "What did he do?"

Son: "I lent him my book on fly fishing and when I asked him to return it he said he already gave it back. But he didn't."

Dad: "So why do you think he said he gave it back?"

Son: "I don't know. Maybe he just wants to keep it. He's had it for almost a year and never returned it. Now I want it back."

Dad: "That's a long time."

Son: "Yeah."

Dad: "How can you get him to return it?"

Son: "I don't see how. He says he doesn't have it anymore. Maybe he forgot where it came from and gave it to somebody else. I don't know."

Dad: "Frustrating."

Son: "It makes me mad."

Dad: "I can imagine."

Son: "It was my favorite fishing book. Grandpa gave it to me. I thought I could trust Jerry with it."

Dad: "I'm sorry it didn't work out. How can you keep something like this from happening again?"

Son: "I'm done letting Jerry borrow my books. He can get his own books from now on."

Dad: "Is this how you want to handle it?"

Son: "Maybe I shouldn't be lending any of my books."

Dad: "They're important to you, aren't they?"

Son: "This one was special. Some of the others I don't care about."

Dad: "So you're saying maybe you won't give out the books that matter."

Son: "Maybe."

Dad: "Do you think this will work for you?"

Son: "People might think I'm stingy. But they're my books. I don't have to let people borrow them."

Dad: "Okay."

Son: "And maybe I'll get another copy of the fly fishing book."

Dad: "Sounds like a great idea."

Tips to optimize the way you guide learning:

- Be on the lookout for everyday experiential learning opportunities.

- When you ask open-ended questions, always let your child do most of the talking. Your job is to listen to make sure you understand what they're telling you.

- Give a copy of the five reflection questions to your child (see Appendix 3, "Learn from Experience"). Encourage them to use it and record their answers in writing.

This chapter in a nutshell:

- **Successes and setbacks happen, but kids don't automatically learn from them.**

- **Coaching a child to learn from what happens to them is a powerful way to create a smarter kid.**

- **You can make sure the learning actually happens by asking five open-ended questions that get at what happened, why, consequences, the lesson, and next steps.**

Learn more about facilitating learning from experience:

- Colin Beard and John P. Wilson, *Experiential Learning*, 4th Ed. (Kogan Page, 2018)

"If what you are doing is not moving you towards your goals, then it's moving you away from your goals."

Brian Tracy

7

....

Get Buy-in for Expectations

How can your child meet your (or their own) expectations if they're not sure what they are? And how can you show appreciation or give constructive feedback if neither you nor your child have defined what's acceptable?

Many parents feel it's their job to "lay down the law," setting boundaries, house rules, and standards for chores. This approach is rarely successful. I talked to a father recently who complained that while his teen daughter "gets it," her teen brother rarely complies with expectations and uses every excuse and stratagem to sidestep them. Your child will be far more enthusiastic about meeting expectations if they're involved in creating them. There are several ways to involve your child when defining expectations:

- **Participative.** If you know your child cares about what's supposed to happen, and if you have time to involve them, their participation to get agreement will create buy-in. Because they help shape the expectation, they'll be more inclined to "own" it and try to live up to it.

- **Permissive.** When your child cares about the outcome, if you trust their judgment, and if you know you can live with any choice they make, you can let them decide what's best. Your role would then be to support your kid's decision.

- **Autocratic.** Sometimes it's not appropriate to ask for input. When safety is at stake, if it's a life-or-death situation, or if the action is critical and there's simply no time to discuss options, just explain what has to be done and why. In addition, if your child doesn't care one way or the other, you can simply inform them of what's expected.

In the end, enthusiasm matters more than compliance. The key is not just establishing clear expectations, but when possible, going one step further: involving your child to create expectations they agree are fair and effective, so they not only understand what should happen, *they want to comply with it.* To get this kind of buy-in, you can discuss expectations with your child. This kind of participative approach is realistic and effective by the time a child enters school.

Recognize the "buy-in moment"

...when faced with a goal, milestone or task, and you expect specific effort or results from your child.

Engage your "buy-in mindset"

My child is more motivated to accomplish a difficult objective if they own it, and so I ask for their input to help frame it.

Scenario #1:

Dad: "You spend too much time with that game console. It's not good for you. From now on you'll be allowed to play games for a half-hour a day, after homework, and one hour a day on weekends."

Son: "But Dad, it's impossible to get anything out of a game in half an hour."

Dad: "I don't care. You need to spend more time outdoors. You could be playing a sport. Or hanging out with friends. You could be reading."

Son: "None of my friends have restrictions like that. It's unfair."

Dad: "You're a teenager now. Your brain needs to develop the critical thinking skills you'll need when you're grown up. Those games may be fun, but they're not only not helping you. In fact, they're probably bad for you."

Son: "But it's *my* game console. You gave it to me for Christmas."

Dad: "Now I'm thinking I made a mistake. Anyway, the rule stands. If you don't comply, I'll have to undo that Christmas present."

Son: "Oh, Dad!"

Scenario #2:

Dad: "You're spending too much time on the game console. I want us to set some reasonable guidelines."

Son: "What for? What's the problem?"

Dad: "Well, you're a teenager now, the time when your brain has the potential to develop some important critical thinking skills. The kind you'll need when you're a grown man, trying to be successful."

Son: "Video games aren't hurting anything."

Dad: "I'd like us to talk about this. I'd like to get your input before we decide what's best."

Son: "Okay. But I don't know what the problem is."

Dad: "I read that these games are realistic and exciting, which I guess is the whole point. But if exposure is prolonged, the excitement can cause chemicals to enter the thinking part of your brain, disrupting the formation of critical thinking skills. And you spend an awful lot of time gaming. These games are designed to be addictive, and I don't want you to get addicted."

Son: "I'm not addicted."

Dad: "I hope not. But you could get that way. You spend hours gaming when you could be outdoors. You could be playing a sport. Or hanging out with your friends. You could be reading."

Son: "But I don't want to give up playing video games. I love the challenge."

Dad: "I don't think you should give it up. Just more moderation. And to tell you the truth, I don't like those shooter games. Pretending to shoot people. I don't like what that could be doing to your brain."

Son: "I only have one shooter game. But what about my strategy games? They could be teaching me to plan and be logical."

Dad: "That's a good point. If you get rid of the shooter game, you could spend more time with the strategy games. I might like to play one of those games with you."

Son: "That would be cool."

Dad: "But we need to cut way back on the time you spend gaming. It would be really good for you to make room for other stuff, like earning money, for example. In a couple years you'll be wanting to borrow the car. If you prove to me that you're responsible, I'll give you the keys. But you'll have to pitch in for gas and the extra insurance."

Son: "Hmm."

Dad: "Seriously, you need to cut back to a moderate level of gaming. What do you think is a fair and healthy limit?"

Son: "How about two hours after school, if I get my homework done first?"

Dad: "That still sounds like too much. You need more balance in your life. I was thinking that a half an hour would be enough."

Son: "Dad, I can't do anything with a game in half an hour."

Dad: "All right. An hour a day, provided your homework is done first. And two hours on weekends."

Son: "I could try that."

Dad: "And after the hour, the game console lives in the kitchen. And we get rid of that shooter game. No more shooter games."

Son: "Okay."

Dad: "Great. So what do you think should happen if you exceed the time limit?"

Son: "Then I lose gaming privileges for a week."

Dad: "That sounds good. For the first offense. Then no games for a month after the second offense."

Son: "Okay."

Dad: "Sounds like we have a deal. I'm counting on you to be a man and live up to your promises. Let's see how it goes."

In the first scenario, Dad took an autocratic approach. He knew his son needed to cut back on time spent gaming, so he exercised his authority and issued a directive. But it wasn't the kind of boundary-setting that would inspire his son to comply.

The first scenario has a "we-they" feel to it. In the second, the son experiences the challenge as "we're in this together." In the second scenario, Dad didn't just lay down the law. Instead, he asked his son for input. They talked about it and together set realistic expectations. This sent a message that Dad respects his son's capacity for being reasonable. By involving him, Dad created the possibility of making changes that improve the situation, and because his son helped shape the expectations, he "bought in" to them.

In short, there's an important difference between setting expectations and getting buy-in for them. If your child has strong feelings about the issue and if you have time to get their input, there's a greater chance your child will be motivated to comply. A typical reaction when trying to establish boundaries is, "That's not fair." You can involve them by asking, *"We need to deal with this. What do you feel would be fair?"* If you listen to understand and engage in dialogue (see Chapter 12, "Engage in Dialogue"), you and your child can hear each other out. When discussing what needs to happen, aim for an expectation that:

- Acknowledges and addresses issues

- Is targeted to achieve the desired end result

- Is acceptable to both you and your child

Clear expectations are the essential first step to later giving feedback about behavior, whether it's appreciation for something done well or constructive feedback when expectations aren't met. In the latter instance, a component of the feedback will be to reaffirm or reset the expectations (see Chapter 10, "Giving Feedback Constructively"). If you can get buy-in for the results you seek, you'll have a greater chance of cooperation.

This chapter in a nutshell:

- **If you want your child to live up to your expectations, they need to know exactly what they are.**

- **Expectations can be ambitious, but they need to be realistic.**

- **When your child is included in the process of setting or adjusting expectations, issues get addressed and they "buy in," which elevates their desire to do what's required.**

Learn more about establishing expectations:

- Sam Kaner, Facilitator's Guide to Participatory Decision-Making (Jossey-Bass, 2014)

- Mel Silberman, PeopleSmart (Barrett-Koehler, 2000), Skill 3

- Jane Healy, How to Have Intelligent and Creative Conversations with Your Kids (Doubleday, 1992)

"At times our own light goes out and is rekindled by a spark from another person. Each of us has cause to think with deep gratitude of those who have lighted the flame within us."

Albert Schweitzer

8

....

Offer Encouragement

Even though kids are a work-in-progress, their current knowledge, skills, values, attitudes and motivation can lead to more learning and achievement. They may also bring a unique set of core strengths, such as patience, self-confidence, persistence, and many others. Such strengths can make them resilient, allowing them to continue giving their best effort in spite of inevitable difficulties. Faced with a setback, kids who believe in themselves and want to succeed eventually recover and continue striving.

On the other hand, a child might be so disheartened that they give up. Imagine a gifted runner who, in the final stretch of a race, trips and falls. In pain, they realize that much of their lead has been lost. If they get back up, they might still have a chance of winning. But will they recover?

Life for a young person can sometimes feel like that. A disappointment, such as a betrayal by a friend, an unkind remark, or a failure in class, can feel so devastating that the child "loses heart." The negatives can seem so overwhelming that they no longer appreciate what's possible, become unsure of themselves, and feel that continuing to strive is not worth the effort.

This is what we call *discouragement*.

When self-encouragement isn't taking hold, you can help. Most people have the idea that offering encouragement is an instinctive act, that if you have a good heart, it comes naturally.

But offering encouragement is actually a special skill, and few parents are practiced in it. What many people think of as encouragement can have the opposite effect.

The classic form of mistaken encouragement is false assurance. "Everything is going to be all right." Has anyone ever said that to you? Even though they may have offered it with a kind spirit, statements like this are empty if they have no basis.

Another way parents sometimes try to encourage is to sugarcoat reality. They may say, "This isn't so bad." Downplaying an unpleasant situation is a common coping mechanism, but anyone who's been brought to their knees by adversity knows that what's bothering them really is this bad, and saying that it isn't doesn't help.

A parent might even take the tough love approach, saying something like, "Come on, stuff happens. Get over it." When this does work, it's usually with particularly strong kids who are already encouraging themselves.

Discouragement happens when an adverse situation causes someone to be so focused on their pain and the negatives that they're no longer acknowledging the positives of their situation—even though the upsides are real and valid. For encouragement to work, the key is to be reality-based. Every situation is a mixture of negative and positive elements: challenges and opportunities; limitations and possibilities; problems and solutions; advantages and disadvantages; strengths and weaknesses; mistakes and lessons learned.

As with any communication skill, the first step is to notice when your child is discouraged and approach them with the right attitude.

Recognize the "encouragement moment"

...when you notice that something has happened to cause your child to be discouraged.

Engage your "encouragement mindset"

My child sometimes doesn't bounce back from adversity right away. I remind them of their strengths, what's possible, and that I want to support them.

When offering encouragement, your task is to help restore a balanced perspective—one that reminds your child about the good in a bad situation. You can use these elements of encouragement in sequence, in any order, or in isolation:

- **Listen with empathy to understand.**

- **Affirm your child's strengths.**

- **Restore perspective.**

- **Offer support.**

Listen with empathy to understand.

Listening is first on this list because when you listen to understand, you learn what happened and what your child is feeling. Even though you might be tempted to rescue them, listening is not about telling them what they should be thinking, feeling and doing. By listening, we mean what I described in Chapter 4 ("Listen to Understand"): focusing your attention, sensing their feelings, listening for the meaning, and checking what you hear.

If you're listening well, your discouraged child may start "venting." You might hear frustration and anger. This is a good sign. When someone expresses negative feelings, it's because they need to. They might even feel relieved afterward. Sometimes, this is all a kid needs to "snap out of it."

Affirm your child's strengths.

Nobody is perfect; everyone is a unique blend of strengths and weaknesses. The idea is to remind your child of their strengths. When things go wrong, kids sometimes feel guilt and blame themselves. They may feel inadequate. They may experience a blow to their self-esteem and self-confidence. They can temporarily lose sight of who they are and what they're capable of.

When kids focus on their shortcomings, they need to be reminded of their strengths. They will probably be focused on the failure at hand, not past achievements; so it can help to remind them that they've succeeded before in equally tough or even tougher situations.

Restore perspective.

In addition to an unbalanced view of themselves, a discouraged child may also focus on the negatives in their situation. That's natural—these are the issues that are causing distress.

To restore a balanced, realistic perspective, acknowledge the negatives, but also remind your child that their situation may not be all negative. While some situations, such as bullying, may not have an upside, often there are advantages, potentials, opportunities, and resources to consider. If so, pointing out these positives can be helpful, because they're real, too.

Offer support.

When your child has been discouraged by difficulty or failure, they may wonder what you think of them. Do you still love them? Do you still believe in them? In light of current setbacks, will you think poorly of them? Now is the time to reassure them that you're still very much in their corner.

Let's take a look at an example of effective encouragement. Notice how Mom senses that encouragement is needed and then applies all the elements:

Mom: "Hey…"

Son: "Mmm…"

Mom: "You don't seem your usual bigger-than-life self today."

Son: "Smaller-than-life is more like it."

Mom: "That doesn't sound good. What's up?"

Son: "You know that internet science project I've been working on for the past three weeks at school?"

Mom: "Uh-huh."

Son: "Well, I got it all done finally and went to demo it for my teacher today, and he told me some other kid is doing something similar, only flashier. He said I should work on something else instead."

Mom: "So your project is history."

Son: "Right. Along with my life for the past three weeks."

Mom: "You put an awful lot into it."

Son: "I did. I really did. And for nothing."

Mom: "No wonder you're bummed out. Sorry, dude."

Son: "Yeah. I wish I'd known this before. I wanted to show what I can do. I wish my teacher had told me earlier. I'm back at square zero. What a waste. I feel like a total fool."

Mom: "No way. You're a smart guy, and now you're even smarter. I bet you learned a lot working on the project."

Son: "Ha. I guess I did. But for what?"

Mom: "Well, for starters, I wonder if your work can be modified and used for a different project."

Son: "What do you mean?"

Mom: "Your project was about genetics. Doesn't it relate to diseases, like cancer?"

Son: "I don't know. I guess so."

Mom: "Couldn't you find out whether there's a connection you can build on?"

Son: "You know, that's interesting."

Mom: "If it's a good match, you could have the solution in days, not weeks. You'll be back on track."

Son: "Maybe. Thanks for the idea, Mom."

Mom: "You bet. Let me know if you need any more brilliant suggestions."

Son: "I will."

What Mom does first is listen. Then she helps her son recover a balanced, realistic perspective of himself and his situation. It's remarkable how kids recover with genuine encouragement.

A few tips for encouraging your child:

- **Help them visualize a positive outcome.** When your child is especially discouraged, try asking a question such as, "If you were to imagine this situation turning out really well, what would that look like?" It's nearly impossible for someone to answer this question without seeing things that could help turn a situation around.

- **Know when to stop encouraging**. While listening, if you sense that your child is beginning to take heart, let them go the rest of the distance without your help. Remember it's always better if someone thinks, *I did this myself*. Sometimes, if you just listen well, it's possible that none of the other elements will be needed. Aim to deliver just the right amount of encouragement to those who need it.

- **Don't wait for discouragement to offer encouragement.** From time to time, offer bits of encouragement while your child is still doing well. Express your appreciation and confidence. This will help keep them strong, so that when the inevitable problems and frustrations happen, their discouragement will be minimal or non-existent. With this kind of "inoculation," a young person can stay strong enough to encourage themselves.

To get your encouragement "reps," stay alert for encouragement moments, such as when your child:

- Has experienced a loss or setback

- Seems unhappy or depressed

- Failed to accomplish a goal

- Has been criticized or bullied

- Is having persistent problems at school

Failures and setbacks can happen to anyone, and it's human nature to feel disappointed and discouraged. Your kid can recover a balanced perspective if you help them acknowledge their strengths and see the positives in their situation.

This chapter in a nutshell:

- **Discouragement is a real possibility for a child who has a full plate.**

- **Not every child recovers from adversity quickly.**

- **You can encourage by reminding your child of their strengths, what's possible, and your willingness to be there with support.**

Learn more about encouragement:

- Larry Crabb, Encouragement: The Unexpected Power of Building Others Up (Zondervan, 2013)

- Mark Goulston, Just Listen (AMACOM, 2015), Chapter 17

"Nothing else can quite substitute for a few well-chosen, well-timed, sincere words of praise. They're absolutely free and worth a fortune."

Sam Walton

"Feeling gratitude and not expressing it is like wrapping a present and not giving it."

William Arthur Ward

9

....

Express Appreciation

Parents are often frustrated by the things kids do. Constantly coping with unwanted behavior usually means that most of the feedback parents give to kids is negative.

This is unfortunate because reinforcing good behavior is much more effective than reacting negatively to things that go wrong. When parents focus on the negatives, kids feel unappreciated. Problems must be addressed, but *most children need a lot more praise than criticism.*

Yes, when kids fight, don't live up to their agreements, or make a half-hearted effort, you need to bring it to their attention. While you need to address these issues, kids may feel that their best efforts go unnoticed, that they get a lot more negative feedback than positive feedback. And this may be true, if you take the good for granted, focusing mostly on problems. The bottom line is that if kids only hear criticism, they may not respond enthusiastically when you point out when you'd like them to try harder.

If you expect good things from your child, you need to continuously build them up, not tear them down.

When parents don't praise their kids often enough, it's usually because they need to make a more consistent effort to "catch them doing things right." It starts with making a habit to look for these opportunities.

Recognize the "appreciation moment"

...when you notice that your child has done something well, made a special effort, or achieved something outstanding.

Engage your "appreciation mindset"

I notice when my child has done their best and affirm them for their effort.

A simple "Thank You!"

It's kind of basic, but saying "Thanks!" is often neglected when you're in a hurry. But when kids feel unappreciated for the good things they do, chances are they'll withhold that extra effort in the future. The recommendation is simple: When they've done what you want them to do, helped you out, or achieved something excellent, don't let the moment pass. Express your genuine gratitude.

*"Jill, **thank you** for clearing away the dishes. I appreciate your help!"*

*"Harry, **thank you** for starting the laundry. I usually do it, but I'm in such a rush today!"*

You get the idea. Just be someone who remembers to say *thanks*. Genuine, heartfelt appreciation is hard to beat.

Positive Feedback

Recognition. Affirmation. Gratitude. Appreciation. Praise. Positive strokes. Pats on the back. Attagirls. Attaboys. All good stuff! It's amazing how motivating a compliment can be. Any kind of acknowledgement of something done well will probably feel good.

But there's a simple approach to positive feedback that works best. Instead of giving a general comment, *mention the specific action that pleased you—and how you feel about it.*

Situation: A child remembers to take out the trash before going to school.

General comment: *"Good job, Joey!"* Or Mom could have said, *"Awesome, Joey."* No harm done. General praise is positive input, so it feels good. At least Joey knows Mom is happy. But when praise is specific, it has double the power.

Specific feedback: *"I appreciate that you remembered to take out the trash. It's a big help to me and no nasty smell in the kitchen!"*

Notice that Mom uses an I-message to express her positive feedback. By being specific, the child knows how Mom feels and exactly what pleased her, so he knows what he needs to do to continue doing it right.

Situation: The daughter does the dishes, even though it's her brother's week to do it.

General feedback: *"You're so sweet!"* Nice! Who wouldn't like to hear that? But praise has more impact when you tell a child how something they did made a difference.

Specific feedback: *"Honey, it meant a lot to me that you did the dishes tonight. Sonny had to leave early, and otherwise it would have been my job to clean up."*

Over time, try to give more positive feedback than negative feedback. The goal isn't to praise every little thing your child does. Children know when they've earned your appreciation and when they haven't, when you're sincere and when you're just going through the motions. Just make a more consistent effort to "catch them doing things right."

Years ago, my friend's daughter, then a senior in high school, was benched on the basketball team. She had been replaced by a bigger, stronger, more talented freshman. She was angry because she felt she had earned the opportunity to start at that position. Her father agreed with her and shared her resentment. Ultimately, she quit the team and pursued horseback riding.

We make choices and create the paths we follow in life, and in this young woman's case, the new path she created gave her joy. But I remember thinking at the time that her dad had missed an opportunity to affirm the hard work she had done on the team and how proud he was of the level of skill she had achieved and the heart she showed every time she was on the court.

Appreciating Appreciation

This chapter has been about expressing appreciation. But when you're on the receiving end, it's just as important to do a good job of receiving it. If you're lucky, someday your child will thank you for something you've done. When it happens, I hope it feels good!

However, if you want those positive strokes to come your way more often, *you want your child to feel good about making you feel good*. When they express their appreciation, you don't want them to think they made a mistake. You want them to feel that their appreciation was appreciated.

I mention this because some people, for a variety of reasons, feel awkward about responding to praise. It's possible they considered what they did to be something they do all the time—not worthy of praise. Sometimes people who don't have strong self-esteem distrust positive input from others. Or maybe they aren't used to receiving praise; it takes them by surprise, and in the moment they don't know what to say.

Keep in mind that appreciation is almost always offered with a good heart, expecting that it will be well received. So if you enjoyed the affirmation and hope it happens again someday, the best response is nothing more than what your own momma told you back when she was teaching you to tie your shoes. She told you to remember to say "you're welcome" when someone says "thank you."

An effective response to appreciation can simply be a version of your momma's advice, offered with sincerity and a smile:

"Thank you, it's nice to be appreciated."

"I'm glad you liked it."

"It's nice to know it helped."

"I appreciate that."

"Your saying that means a lot."

The key is to make sure you don't let the opportunity pass you by. Even if you feel a little embarrassed by praise, always express your appreciation for being appreciated. You'll be encouraging positive feedback; and every home needs more of that!

A few tips for making positive feedback more effective:

- **Commit to offering positive feedback more often than you give constructive feedback.** This may mean establishing a new habit: catching your child doing things right. You already notice when things displease you; your discomfort signals you nearly every time. Noticing effort and achievement is different. You'll need to make an effort. Make it a goal to affirm your child at least twice as often as you give constructive feedback.

- **Give positive feedback only when they've earned it.** Contrary to what some "experts" suggested years ago, piling on the praise isn't always better. You might get away with unearned praise once; but kids will quickly catch on, and this kind of praise can backfire. If your child senses you're insincere, they might question your motives and discount your praise when it is sincere.

- **Praise a strong effort, even if it fails.** When an outstanding effort fails to lead to success, there's a danger that a child will self-criticize. But that level of effort may well achieve success in the future. If you hope to see it repeated, let them know you appreciate their effort! For example: *"I thought your report was really good. You spent a lot of time on it, and I loved your emphasis on animal behavior."*

- **On occasion, let them know you appreciate who they are.** Kids who have strong self-esteem and self-confidence are more likely to stand up for themselves and resist peer pressure. But sometimes they can be self-critical. They have talents and strengths, but they may not acknowledge this. So ask about their life, listening deeply, and pointing out *specifically* the best aspects of who they are. For example: *"It means a lot to me that you always tell me the truth."* Avoid generalities such as *"You're really smart,"* which don't communicate the potential of a young person to continue learning and growing.

- **Do it with feeling.** Make sure your child knows you really mean it. If you genuinely feel gratitude and appreciation, let your facial expressions, tone of voice, and nonverbal gestures communicate it.

This chapter in a nutshell:

- The goal of appreciation is to help your child build motivation and confidence to do something outstanding.

- Most parents tend to give corrective feedback more often than expressing appreciation.

- Positive feedback is a much stronger motivator than negative feedback, and you probably should express it more often.

- You need to get good at "catching your kid doing things right."

- The key to high-impact praise is to be specific about what your child did and how you feel about it.

- In addition to affirming achievement and success, show appreciation for outstanding effort, even when it doesn't achieve the hoped-for results.

- Let your child know you understand, appreciate and value them.

Learn more about expressing praise and appreciation:

- Thomas Gordon, *Parent Effectiveness Training* (Three Rivers, 2000)

- Marshall Goldsmith, *What Got You Here Won't Get You There* (Hyperion, 2007), Chapter 10

"We all need people who will give us feedback. That's how we improve."

Bill Gates

10

....

Give Feedback Constructively

School is tough. Adolescence is tough. Life is tough. This is obvious to parents, and most of them say they want their kids to grow up to be resilient. But sometimes an upset parent will react to a child's troubling behavior in a way that defeats this purpose.

Seemingly, it has always been so. Have you ever read *Anne Frank: The Diary of a Young Girl*? This classic is the journal of a middle-school-age Jewish girl whose family was forced to hide from Nazi German soldiers who had conquered Holland during World War II. She survived long enough to leave behind her remarkable diary, but her life ended tragically.

Not many readers have noticed that a major theme of her entries was her complaints about how the adults around her criticized her. "If I talk, everyone thinks I'm showing off, when I'm silent they think I'm ridiculous, rude if I answer, sly if I get a good idea, lazy if I'm tired, selfish if I eat a mouthful more than I should, stupid, cowardly, crafty, etc. The whole day long I hear nothing else but that I am an insufferable baby, and although I laugh about it and pretend not to take any notice, I *do* mind." Of course, her family was in a uniquely stressful situation, and emotions often ran high. But still, as a consequence of how she was treated, Anne distanced herself from her parents, especially her mother.

One night, her mother offered to say prayers with her, and Anne refused. "I felt sorry for Mummy, very, very sorry, because I had seen for the first time in my life that she minds my coldness. I saw the look of sorrow on her face when she spoke of love not being forced. It is hard to speak the truth, and yet it is the truth: she herself has pushed me away, her tactless remarks and her crude jokes, which I don't find at all funny, have now made me insensitive to any love from her side."

Now, in the 21st century, this dynamic still plays out. When a parent is irritated by a child's behavior, their way of reacting can push them further away. In this example, Dad appears in his daughter's bedroom doorway:

Dad: "Your mother called out to you for the third time."

Daughter: "I know. I'm not hungry."

Dad: "Why didn't you answer her the first time?"

Daughter: "I don't know."

Dad: "Do you think I like hearing your mother call for you over and over?"

Daughter: "No."

Dad: "Okay, I'm going to make this simple. I don't care if you're hungry or not. When your mother calls you, you answer her right away. You understand?"

Daughter: *Gives dad a shocked look.*

Dad: "I said, do you understand?"

Daughter: "Yes sir."

Dad: "Good. Now get into the kitchen and find out what she wants."

This is how caring, supportive parents sometimes talk to their kids. They love their children and have high hopes for them. They take raising a family seriously and are doing the best they know how. But despite their good intentions, when they're displeased, parents often react emotionally or from a position of authority, which defeats their purpose. In the above scenario, the father asks a sarcastic question and then issues a series of commands. Communicating this way can be hurtful. It can attack a kid's self-esteem, damage the parent's credibility, and alienate the child:

"What's wrong with you?"

"How many times do I have to tell you…?"

"You should be ashamed of yourself."

"That was dumb. You know that, right?"

"Why don't you do what you're told?"

"That was a terrible thing to do."

"You're acting like a child."

"I can't take any more of this."

"How could you do that?"

"Sometimes I don't know what to do with you."

"Your older brother would never have done something like that."

"Why don't you act your age?"

"What did you think you were doing?"

I came from a family of eight kids, so I heard some of these classics while growing up. (Umm, not directed at me, of course.) When one of us was careless, made mistakes or showed poor judgment, my parents would sometimes react emotionally. I can tell you that in our family these attempts to correct unwanted behavior rarely had the desired effect.

Kids need feedback. They need to know what they're doing well so they can do it more often. And they need to know when their behavior is causing problems, so they can make an effort to change. The spirit of parent-child feedback needs to be encouraging and supportive, so it helps a child grow stronger and more competent.

To be effective, feedback needs to be delivered in an encouraging way.

As with any communication skill, you need to notice when it's needed and approach it with the right attitude.

Recognize the "feedback moment"

...when your child's behavior has come up short and you want to inspire them to do better.

Engage your "feedback mindset"

When I'm not happy with my child's behavior, I share how I feel about it in a positive, encouraging way.

I-Messages

In his book, *Parent Effectiveness Training*, Thomas Gordon introduces a powerful approach he calls the "I-Message." The I-message is simply a phrase in which you use the pronoun "I" to *own your feedback*. For example, you might say, *"I'm disappointed that you haven't done your laundry this week."* Saying it this way is powerful because it states two things that can't be argued:

- What you specifically observed about your child's behavior

- How you feel about it

Implied in the following I-message is an *expectation*, a standard of behavior previously agreed upon between parent and child:

"We've agreed that you'll do your laundry each week, on Sunday afternoon, unless you arrange for an alternate day. Can I count on you to do that?"

When you and your child agree to an expectation, it sets up the possibility for future feedback, after you've observed them in action. You can share *constructive feedback* when the expected behavior isn't met. Or you can share *positive feedback* when you've noticed your child making an effort. I-messages are important elements in both kinds of feedback, the goal of which is to encourage future success.

Constructive Feedback

It's not easy to be a kid. Even teenagers, who are adults-in-process, are in an awkward "in-between" period of life that persists for the better part of a decade. Kids are often confused, inexperienced, and unsure of themselves. They can lose sight of the big picture or misunderstand what's expected. But criticism and hurtful remarks cause resentment, and looking the other way doesn't guide them to correct the unwanted behavior. If their self-esteem is fragile and regularly assaulted, they can become susceptible to peer pressure, which can get them in trouble. In the heat of a moment, a frustrated mom or dad might react with a harsh put-down.

Mom: "Hey, didn't you wear that shirt to school yesterday?"

Son: "I guess so."

Mom: "And the day before that, right?"

Son: "Yeah, so...?"

Mom: "Isn't it pretty smelly by now?"

Son: *No reply.*

Mom: "Well, it's your shirt. If you want to be a slob, I guess it's up to you."

Dad finds his son in the kitchen drinking a soda.

Dad: "I thought you said you were going to wash the car."

Son: "I did."

Dad: "Then how come it's still dirty?"

Son: "What do you mean?"

Dad: "I mean it's still dirty! The bottom of the doors still have road dirt on them. And the grill is covered with bugs."

Son: "Well, I washed it."

Dad: "Well, you did a half-assed job."

Son: "Ah, Dad..."

Dad: "Don't 'Ah, Dad' me. Get back out there and do it right. You need to learn that in life you have to pay attention to what you're doing and not just go through the motions. You know the difference, don't you?"

Son: *Gives Dad a look of resentment, slowly stands up and heads for the door.*

Dad: "Don't make me send you back out there a second time."

Son: "Okay, okay."

Without realizing its impact, the mother implies that her son is a "slob." When talking to his son, Dad initiates an argument and then delivers a lecture, questioning his son's intelligence. Still, it's important to hold up a mirror to a growing child's problem behavior, because they don't always know whether they're doing something right. And if there are serious consequences, you need to help them get back on track while holding them accountable.

Fortunately, it's possible to point out issues in a way that a child will accept. During the past several decades, experts in interpersonal communication have developed a well-tested approach to giving constructive feedback that gets the job done without giving offense. The approach involves five steps:

1. **Affirm the good.**

2. **Describe *specifically* the problem behavior.**

3. **Explain its impact.**

4. **Reset expectations.**

5. **Encourage and offer support.**

Step 1: Affirm the good.

You don't want to sugar-coat or downplay your feedback; but if you only mention the unwanted behavior, it can make your child think you don't notice the good things they do. If your feedback only mentions the negatives, they'll think you're being unfair and discount the rest of what you say. They may even argue with you. To defuse their defensiveness, before you start talking about what bothers you, mention at least one thing related to the actions at hand that you appreciate. For example:

"Ginger, I know that most of the time you're really thoughtful about what you say to your brother."

Step 2: Describe *specifically* the problem behavior.

A behavior isn't the same as values, attitudes, opinions or feelings. A behavior is something you can observe. In this step, you describe precisely what your child did—and only what they did—phrased as an I-message. Put the description in context: how it violated an agreement, norms, or values. Do this without emotion and without making assumptions about intentions. Here's an example of a specific behavior description:

"I overheard what you said to Bobby. You made fun of the way he talks."

Step 3: Explain its impact.

Describe the consequences of the behavior, even—if appropriate—your feelings about it, such as surprise, concern, disappointment, etc.

"I could tell by looking at his face that it hurt his feelings."

At this point, your child may try to explain. *This is an important "listening moment,"* so be prepared to engage your "listen to understand" skills. Anything else could cause a rational conversation to escalate to an emotional one.

Ginger: "He makes fun of me sometimes."

You: "You don't like it when he does that and you wanted to get back at him."

Ginger: "Yeah."

You: "You're usually very kind, but it seems like this time you forgot to take his feelings into account."

Ginger: "I guess so."

Step 4: Reset expectations:

Ask for the behavior you want, and explain why. If the action had a serious consequence, discuss ways to make amends. This will create a way for your child to "make things right again." Get agreement on future behavior (see Chapter 7, "Get Buy-in for Expectations"); if you sense they aren't sure what's expected, you can make suggestions. If the situation they caused wasn't that serious, simply conclude by reaffirming the behavior you need.

You: "You remember the golden rule: do unto others as you would have them do unto you. Even if someone isn't nice to you, the right thing to do is to be kind to them rather than getting back at them."

Ginger: "I know. I guess he just made me mad. But that's no excuse. I think I'll tell him I'm sorry."

Step 5: Encourage and offer support.

Always sandwich the meat of constructive feedback between two positives. In addition to your affirmation in Step 1, conclude your feedback by expressing confidence in your child's ability to do the right thing, and confirm your support.

"That would be great. I appreciate your kindness, your positive attitude, and your willingness to make your brother feel better."

Tips for making constructive feedback more encouraging:

- **Calm down first.** When you're upset with your child's behavior, you can avoid saying something emotional, aggressive, or sarcastic by simply saying nothing while you let your emotions subside. Your goal is to encourage someone to behave differently, not to vent or create defensiveness or resentment. If you say something hurtful, your child won't believe you mean well.

- **Don't hold it inside.** Giving constructive feedback is never easy, and for this reason, parents sometimes decide not to say anything. But if you need your kid to make more of an effort, don't put off bringing it up. If you let your discontent stew, eventually you'll need to address so many past instances that they won't be able to deal with all of them. And chances are you'll feel the need to express feelings that have mounted up over time.

- **Only address issues your child can do something about.** Sometimes the thing that displeases you is beyond your kid's ability to fix, so confronting them with it will be pointless and unfair.

- **Be sure of your facts.** Otherwise, the focus of your feedback could be in error, in which case it will be discounted. The best approach is to stick to behavior you've observed personally. If someone else complains, you'll need to check facts with them and make their account part of your feedback.

- **Focus on only one issue at a time.** Feedback is successful if your child later makes an effort to change behavior. Addressing more than one issue at a time is usually more than a kid can handle.

- **Think about what you'll say.** Before you speak, take a moment to remember the five basic elements of constructive feedback:

1. Affirm the good.

2. Describe specifically the problem behavior.

3. Explain its impact.

4. Reset expectations.

5. Encourage and offer support.

Mentally rehearse, so you say the most effective things in the most effective sequence.

- **Give feedback while the incident is still fresh (within 24 hours).** If you don't address the issue in a timely way, your child may not remember exactly what happened and may wonder why you waited so long to bring it up.

- **Keep your feedback private and confidential.** Respect your child's needs and feelings. If you embarrass them in front of others, you'll create resentment, which will diminish their motivation to change.

- **Check that your child is ready to receive feedback.** Ask if this is a good time to talk about the incident. For a variety of reasons, they may not be ready to consider what you have to say. If so, you can say, *"That's fine. We can talk about it later."*

- **Mention specific actions and behaviors.** If you present evidence or talk about actions you've observed, it's hard for your child to deny or challenge you. Don't mention values, attitudes, personality or other factors which you can't observe directly.

- **If your child responds, listen to understand.** You may learn more about the circumstances, which could affect how you reset your expectations.

- **Be honest.** Tell it like it is. Don't sugar-coat your description of the behavior, even if delivering it makes you feel uncomfortable.

- **Be sincere.** Don't just say the words as if they were part of a formula. Stick to the facts and how you feel about them.

- **Own your feedback—use "I-statements."** If the behavior displeases you, say so. Don't say, "Your father isn't going to like it."

This chapter in a nutshell:

- **The purpose of constructive feedback is to tell your child about their problem behavior in an encouraging way, so you build them up instead of tear them down.**

- **Constructive feedback should be positive. Sandwich your feedback with an affirmation on the front end and encouragement at the end.**

- **Using I-statements, your feedback should acknowledge the good they do, describe your child's problem behavior specifically, reveal the impact it had on you and others, reset expectations, and offer encouragement and support.**

- **Be accurate, sincere, thoughtful, and respectful when giving feedback.**

Learn more about giving constructive feedback:

- Rick Maurer, *Feedback Toolkit* (Productivity Press, 1994)

- Marshall Goldsmith, *What Got You Here Won't Get You There* (Hyperion, 2007), Chapter 6

"Treat every piece of advice as a gift."

Marshall Goldsmith

"Feedback is the breakfast of champions."

Rick Tate

11

....

Accept Feedback Graciously

Chapter 10 ("Give Feedback Constructively") affirmed the value of giving constructive feedback. In this chapter, I reverse the situation and focus on how to respond when *you're* the one receiving the feedback.

Even poorly communicated feedback—criticism—is worth its weight in gold, if you accept it with a gracious spirit. The reason is simple: no one is perfect, and most people have blind spots. You may not see yourself the way your family sees you, and you could be doing things that are detrimental to your relationship with them.

If you're like most people, you learned to communicate "on the street," so to speak. You acquired your way of interacting not from formal instruction and professional coaching, but from family and friends. So it's possible that some of them may be put off by one or more of your habitual ways of relating to them. It could be anything: a formal or distancing demeanor, a habit of expressing impatience, a failure to notice their good behavior, or a lack of interest in their activities. The consequence of unintended slights or dysfunctional behavior can be a loss of intimacy, trust, and motivation.

Feedback can hold a mirror to your behavior, informing you about problems and issues you weren't aware of, the kind of awareness that can help you do something about it. Most kids are reluctant to offer their parents feedback, because they aren't sure how to phrase it and they aren't sure how the parent will take it. This is why you should consider any feedback you get "a gift," even if it sounds like a complaint or criticism.

An important question: *If you're lucky enough to get some constructive feedback, what are the chances it will be offered again in the future?*

The answer is simple: *100%, if you accept the feedback graciously.*

Recognize the "accept feedback graciously moment"

...when your child has given you feedback and you want to encourage this kind of input in the future.

Engage your "accept feedback graciously mindset"

I ask for feedback, and when my child gifts me with it in any form, I listen without reacting, thank them, and follow up with an effort to change my behavior.

The purpose of this chapter is to outline what experts have said about accepting feedback in a way that reassures your child that it was received in the best possible way. Here are five things you can—and should—do that will assure your child that you're genuinely open to receiving feedback:

- **Ask for feedback.**
- **Listen without being defensive.**
- **Apologize.**
- **Thank your child for their feedback.**
- **Follow up.**

Ask for feedback.

Typically, feedback is given unsolicited. But what if you don't wait to be surprised with it? What if you *ask for it?*

> *"It's important to me that I'm giving you the support you need. There are times when I wish I had handled things differently. So when you feel I haven't been a great parent, I'd like you to tell me how I could do better. Please give me your honest feelings about it. I promise to take you seriously."*

Imagine the impact saying something like this would have on your child's perceptions of you.

Listen without being defensive, apologize, and express gratitude.

Most people feel blindsided by feedback. This causes them to make a classic mistake: they try to defend themselves. This is a natural emotional reaction. Criticism—or even well-stated encouraging feedback—never feels good. In fact, it may feel as though you're underappreciated and the feedback is unfair. You may want to justify your behavior or even deny what you're hearing.

If you respond with defensiveness, though, you'll send the message that their feedback was rejected. Put yourself in your kid's shoes. Given that giving you feedback is difficult for them, if you try to argue or defend your behavior, what do you think will be the likelihood of receiving this kind of helpful input in the future?

Suppress your defensiveness. Whenever you receive any kind of feedback, the most important thing you can do is listen to what they say without trying to justify your behavior. Think of this as an absolute rule. Defensiveness will damage your ability to internalize the feedback and discourage feedback in the future.

Listen to understand. Do this instead of getting defensive. Focus your attention and listen without speaking until you think you know what they're trying to say. Then check the message (see Chapter 4, "Listen to Understand"). In the process, you can identify specifically what they'd like to see more of.

Then apologize. Marshall Goldsmith says this about accepting feedback graciously: "I regard apologizing as the most magical, healing, restorative gesture human beings can make." Many people feel that owning up to a mistake will damage how they're perceived. This is a horrible misconception. The opposite is true: your child is already aware of your issue and an apology communicates that you recognize it and genuinely want to make amends.

Finally, thank them. Once you're sure you know what the issue is, express your appreciation for their feedback.

Daughter: "I hate it when you always remind me to do my homework."

You: "I guess I do that."

Daughter: "It's like you don't trust me to do it."

You: "I see that. I should probably just let you take care of your own business."

Daughter: "Yeah. I don't always do it right away, but I always get to it."

You: "I'm sorry I've been so bossy. You're so smart and I want you to do well. I'll try to do better, just trust you to do what you need to do."

Daughter: "Thanks, Mom."

Follow up.

After accepting your feedback graciously, you need to follow through on your promises. If you committed to demonstrating a new behavior, now you need to deliver.

Also, along the way you can ask for more feedback. Or even better, ask for what Marshall Goldsmith calls "feedforward." If this concept is new to you, think of feedforward as getting input related to future behavior, while feedback is related to what happened in the past. All you need to do is ask for suggestions to improve an aspect of your behavior. For example:

"Lately, I've been trying to be more supportive of your friendships. Could you suggest some ways I can improve how I do that?"

Suppressing your defensiveness, listening to understand, apologizing, expressing gratitude, and asking for feedforward—these aren't the typical reactions of a parent to feedback! This is a significant paradigm shift. It may be difficult for you to put this new approach into practice; but if you want your child to continue giving you the gift of feedback, it's important for you to convey to them that it's worth the effort.

This chapter in a nutshell:

- **Most parents react defensively to constructive feedback.**

- **Doing so will discourage your child from sharing honest feedback with you.**

- **Accepting feedback graciously will convince them it was worth the effort.**

- **The paradigm shift: suppress defensiveness, listen to understand, apologize, express gratitude, follow through, and ask for feedforward.**

Learn more about accepting feedback:

- Marshall Goldsmith, *What Got You Here Won't Get You There* (Hyperion, 2007), Chapters 7, 11, and 12

- Joe Folkman, *Turning Feedback into Change* (Novations, 1996)

"You never really understand a person until you consider things from his point of view....until you climb into his skin and walk around in it."

Harper Lee

"When you talk, you are only repeating what you already know. But if you listen, you may learn something new."

Dalai Lama

12

....

Engage in Dialogue

Do you remember when your child was a toddler? Amazingly cute, and in terms of knowing how the world works, amazingly innocent. A few years later, they were in school, and thanks to you and their teachers (and maybe some of their friends) they started to figure a few things out. Even when kids begin high school, there's still so much they don't know, though hopefully they're continuing to learn and form opinions. In the best case, they can also get smarter by talking with you—not by listening to lectures on your view of life, but by sharing thoughts, ideas, and opinions. You won't always agree with what you hear, but at least you'll hear it; and they'll hear you. This kind of non-argumentative conversation is called "dialogue."

When I was a teenager, I learned not to disagree with my dad. For reasons I've never fully understood, the few times I expressed a contrary point of view—when I was old enough to feel confident that I had something to say—he physically attacked me. He never hurt me, because I was able to dodge him until he calmed down. Maybe he felt that as the father, his intelligence shouldn't be challenged by his son. Or it could have been that as a young man, I wasn't very tactful. In any case, I learned to keep my opinions to myself. And his reactions created a distance between us that was never fully bridged.

When you and your child clash, it may not be that they want something you consider unacceptable. It may simply be that the two of you have different opinions about something.

Disagreeing with your child can be a discomforting experience. Questioning one of your long-held beliefs could mean questioning a whole set of related beliefs. Being confronted with an opposing opinion could make you feel defensive. Or you may sense that your child's opinions could lead to trouble.

The way most people deal with disagreements is to argue or debate—to prove that they're right. If you're like most parents, you believe your adult point of view is better informed, backed by more education, and based on more life experience. And you're probably right on all counts.

Say for example, Mom is in the passenger seat with her teen driver:

Mom: "Honey, you didn't signal just now when you changed lanes."

Daughter: "It's okay, Mom, there were no cars around."

Mom: "But it's the law. You need to signal before you move from one lane into another."

Daughter: "It was safe, Mom. I checked. I always check first."

Mom: "I know, but isn't that like saying it's okay to roll past a stop sign because no cars were around? I worry that someday you'll be in a hurry and you won't see something and you'll have an accident."

Daughter: "I've done it a hundred times and nothing has happened. It's okay."

Mom: "Honey, it's not okay. For your own safety, you need to follow all the laws, not just whenever you feel like it."

Daughter: "It's silly to signal when there's no one to see it."

Mom: "It's a bad habit. Someday you'll be in a hurry and you'll change lanes without signaling and you'll hit a car you didn't see."

Daughter: "That won't happen, Mom. I'm careful. You should just trust me."

Mom: "How can I trust you with our car when you don't respect the law?"

Mom and daughter have two different points of view, and neither one is convincing the other. This argument can only heat up until Mom plays the power card. She'll win the argument—technically, anyway. But her daughter is likely to:

- Resent being proved wrong

- Suffer a blow to her self-esteem

- Quietly reject mom's superior point of view

- Feel wary about sharing ideas with her mom in the future

This is why winning an argument with your kid can feel strangely like losing.

The alternative to arguing is dialogue—a structured way of examining issues from different perspectives. Instead of defending your point of view, you openly consider whether there may be more to the issue than you've already considered. Instead of arguing or debating, you engage in a conversation simply to learn what your child believes, and why—and to share your own thoughts on the subject.

When you disagree with your child, share your thinking and learn how your child thinks, without trying to prove you're right and they're wrong.

Recognize the "dialogue moment"

...when you realize that you don't agree with your child's point of view.

Engage your "dialogue mindset"

My child and I may disagree, but we're entitled to our opinions. Without trying to win an argument, I keep an open mind and make an effort to learn why my child has this opinion.

The classic approach to dialogue has several elements:

1. **State your opinion.**
2. **Describe the facts and assumptions upon which your opinion is based.**
3. **Explain your reasoning.**
4. **Encourage the other person to examine your thinking.**
5. **Ask them to share their opinion, facts, assumptions, and reasoning.**

Step 1: State your opinion.

When you initiate dialogue, it's a good idea to acknowledge that your opinion is, well, an opinion. The purpose of this all-important step is to set aside the message, *I know I'm right*. Your opinions are important because they're the framework upon which you base many of your decisions. But opinions aren't final truths. Instead, they're always tentative conclusions based on available facts and assumptions. Since everyone doesn't share the same opinions, some of them may be founded on better facts and assumptions. Therefore, you stand to learn something when you consider the facts, assumptions, and conclusions of others.

> *"I see we don't agree on this. That's fine. Would you be open to our exchanging ideas about it? I don't want to argue or try to convince you I'm right. I'd just like to explain where I'm coming from and learn about your point of view. If it's OK with you, I'll go first. Here's my take...."*

Step 2: Describe the facts and assumptions upon which your opinion is based.

Opinions aren't facts, but they may be based on facts. However, a single fact doesn't necessarily make a strong case. Forming an opinion without considering enough factual evidence is called "jumping to conclusions."

> *"You see, I've always thought that...."*

> *"And according to an article I read...."*

> *"In my experience, I've observed that...."*

> *"When I was in school, my favorite teacher told me...."*

Step 3: Explain your reasoning.

While personal feelings, instinct and intuition can guide your decision-making, it's important to ask whether your opinion makes sense. Is your opinion well supported by facts? Is your reasoning sound?

> *"So based on what these experts say and my own experience, I've concluded that most of the time...."*

Step 4: Encourage your child to examine your facts and reasoning.

To promote dialogue, ask your child what he or she thinks about the opinions, assumptions, facts and reasoning you've shared.

Again, listen to understand what's going on in your child's mind. Resist the impulse to defend your opinions. Just give their evaluation consideration.

"That's where I'm coming from anyway. Do you have any thoughts about what I just said?"

Step 5: Ask your child to share their assumptions, facts, and reasoning.

Now it's your child's turn to open up about their ideas–and time for you to listen. Are you willing to keep an open mind? Or are you so opposed to your child's position on the issue that you feel compelled to lecture or prove them wrong? Be prepared to listen simply to understand. As you listen, ask yourself, *Why do they think that?* If you feel defensiveness or other negative reactions, set them aside, so you can learn what's going on in your child's head.

Ask questions to discover the same three things you just shared:

1. **Their opinions.** Try to discover what your child believes. If you hear something you didn't expect or something that conflicts with your own opinion, be careful not to get defensive.

   "Now that you know where I'm coming from, what's your opinion?"

2. **Facts and assumptions on which they base these opinions.** When you hear an opinion, ask how they came to that opinion. If they offer evidence, ask if they have more. Take care that your tone of voice comes across as genuine curiosity, not a challenge.

   "I'm curious how you came to that conclusion. Was there something specific that you've read or heard?"

3. **Their reasoning.** As you listen, you'll pick up on the reasoning behind their arguments. Summarize this reasoning to be sure you understand it.

"It sounds like you're saying this based on...and you've concluded that...."

As your child explains their point of view, you should listen to the best of your ability. In the above example, the parent shared their point of view first. It's equally effective to begin by asking about the child's point of view.

The purpose of dialogue is not to expose the flaws in your child's opinions or to teach your kid a better way of thinking. You engage in this kind of exchange to discover what the two of you believe—and why. That's all. Let your child decide what to do with what you shared.

As for what they share, are you humble enough to consider the possibility of learning something new from your child? When you share ideas with your child, you deal with them on an adult-to-adult basis. Only good things come from taking this approach. You begin to find out how their mind works, who they are, and who they're becoming. And they learn more about you, while discovering that it's okay to be honest with you. They discover what opinions really are and the possibility of adopting more valid opinions. This is a far more valuable outcome than proving that you're right and your child is wrong.

Let's revisit the differences of opinion between Mom and her daughter. When they arrive at their destination, Mom initiates a dialogue:

Mom: "Before we go in, can we just sit here for a minute? I want to talk about changing lanes."

Daughter: "Uh...okay, Mom."

Mom: "You said you think it's safe to change lanes without signaling if you see no other cars around."

Daughter: "Yeah."

Mom: "Why do you think that?"

Daughter: "Well, why should I signal if no one is there to see it? If there are cars around, naturally I would signal."

Mom: "So for you, this is a valid exception to traffic law."

Daughter: "It makes sense to me. There's no chance of an accident."

Mom: "I understand where you're coming from. And you're right, it does make sense. I'd like to share my thoughts about changing lanes. Would that be okay?"

Daughter: "Sure."

Mom: "In my opinion, it's a rule designed to save lives. So I respect it. But mainly, I think signaling even if no one is around creates the right habit. I worry that someday you'll quickly change lanes, not seeing someone in your blind spot."

Daughter: "Mom, that will never happen. I'm careful."

Mom: "I know you are, Sweetheart. I am, too. But can I tell you about something that happened to me?"

Daughter: "Okay."

Mom: "One day several years ago I was on the Interstate on the way to an appointment and traffic was stopped in my lane. I was getting frustrated because the left lane was flowing free. I thought I was going to be late, so I quickly moved the car toward the left lane, and immediately I heard a loud honking and I instinctively veered back into the right lane. I had narrowly avoided crashing into an oncoming car. And you know what? It was a highway patrol car! I felt scared and humiliated, but the officer just frowned and shook his head and kept going. He must have had another emergency. I'm a safe driver, but my impatience almost caused a bad accident."

Daughter: "Scary."

Mom: "I wanted to share that with you because I fear that if something like that could happen to me, a safe driver, it could happen to anyone. It could even happen to you. I'd like to share one more thought."

Daughter: "What?"

Mom: "While I agree with you that no harm is done by not signaling with no cars around, I think there's value in doing it anyway, to repeatedly just do it until it becomes second nature. In other words, creating a habit of signaling anyway could be what saves your life in a bizarre circumstance someday."

Daughter: "I see what you're saying."

Mom: "In the end, you'll always be the one to make the call. It's dangerous out there, and I just want you to be safe, no matter what."

Tips for optimizing the way you engage in dialogue:

- **Make a commitment to avoiding arguments.** Disagreements are inevitable; they happen often and the instinct to react with authority is deeply ingrained. To sense the dialogue moment in time to avoid an argument will be tricky, and you'll have to make a concentrated effort.

- **Study the dialogue framework.** The dialogue approach has been around for decades, but to my knowledge it's never been recommended for parents. Which is strange, when you consider how often parents argue with their kids and the harm arguing does to a relationship. Again, because the skill is probably new to you, you'll need to make a special effort to learn it and begin practicing it.

- **Focus on the benefits.** Even if you know you're right most of the time, you can learn a lot about your "adult-in-progress" by sharing ideas without trying to prove you're right. Also, allowing them to consider your ideas in an adult-adult non-argumentative manner will demonstrate that you respect them and that you really do want to understand them. This is how dialogue can help your relationship.

To get your "reps," stay alert for dialogue moments like these:

- You disagree with something your child said
- Your child expresses an opinion that's not consistent with your values
- Something your child has said has surprised or shocked you
- Your child says something that's inconsistent with facts
- Your child expresses an opinion that could lead to trouble

This chapter in a nutshell:

- **You may disagree with your child, but arguments are counterproductive.**
- **The goal of dialogue is to avoid arguments and debates by learning about your child's thinking.**
- **To initiate dialogue, share your opinion, facts, assumptions, and reasoning.**

- **Or you could start by asking your child about their opinion, facts, assumptions, and reasoning.**

- **Don't pursue dialogue to prevail over your child's opinion. Make it your goal to understand where they're coming from.**

Learn more about dialogue:

- William Isaacs, *Dialogue* (Random House, 2008)

- Marie-Eve Marchand, *The Spirit of Dialogue in a Digital Age* (Dialogue Publications, 2019)

"Unless both sides win, no agreement can be permanent."

Jimmy Carter

13

....

Resolve Conflict Creatively

Disagreements and conflicts are similar: you and your child are at odds with each other. But while a disagreement involves a difference of opinions, conflicts are about action, when your child wants something you consider unacceptable.

Inevitably, your child will want to do something you feel you can't go along with. You'll both feel justified in demanding what you want, a struggle that could create anger and resentment and possibly damage your relationship.

There are many ways to resolve conflicts. Over the years, the most helpful reference I've found for understanding and using conflict resolution strategies is the Thomas-Kilmann model, designed by psychologists Kenneth Thomas and Ralph Kilmann. It compares five approaches, each combining two elements: "assertiveness" (trying to get what you want) with "cooperativeness" (trying to help the other person get what they want). Using the two elements (to a high or low degree) results in five different ways to resolve conflict, each with its own rationale, advantages, and disadvantages:

1. **Competing** (high assertiveness and low cooperativeness). In this approach, you seek a **win-lose** resolution. As the person with the power, you may get what you want, but at the expense of your child, who fails to get what they want. The disadvantage to winning this way is

that it can come to seem like losing, because it creates ill will and could drive your child to seek other undesirable solutions. However, this could be a necessary approach if it means protecting your rights or the safety of your child or defending an all-important priority.

2. **Accommodating** (low assertiveness and high cooperativeness). This is considered a **lose-win** approach because instead of trying to get what you want, you give in to the wants of your child. Accommodating could take the form of generosity. Or you could give in if doing so promotes good will, and what you give up isn't that important to you. But you don't want to give in just to avoid conflict, because doing so might later have bad consequences for your child.

3. **Avoiding** (low assertiveness and low cooperativeness). This is the **lose-lose** approach. You simply refuse to deal with the conflict. Because neither you nor your child gets their needs met, this approach can allow the conflict to fester and gather intensity. On the other hand, avoiding the conflict can push resolving it into the future, if doing so avoids danger or dealing with the issue later promises a better chance of success.

4. **Compromising** (Moderate assertiveness and moderate cooperativeness). I consider this a **win-lose—win-lose** approach, because both parties get something but at the cost of giving up something they need. It's the "something is better than nothing" approach. It might mean splitting the difference, some give-and-take, or seeking a resolution in the middle ground. Partially satisfying the needs may resolve the conflict, but perhaps only temporarily, because what has been given up may remain as an unsatisfied need.

5. **Collaborating** (high assertiveness and high coopera-tiveness). This is the **win-win** resolution—the opposite of avoiding. When two people are in conflict, they back off their initial demands and instead focus on their needs. They then entertain other possible solutions that meet both their needs. This approach requires mutual respect, a willingness to listen, and creativity to find so-lutions.

While there may be situations where any of these could be the most effective strategy, most of the time my favorite is No. 5—*collaborating,* because it seeks to satisfy the needs of both parties. This option is a way for both kids and their parents to get their needs met, not by getting their initial demands, but by exploring alternate solutions.

The key is for both you and your kid to back off your initial wants and instead focus on the needs that are driving the wants, and then creatively search for other solutions that will address your needs and your child's needs at the same time.

The next time you're nose-to-nose with your child, instead of giving in or relying on your parental authority to get your way, consider the win-win approach. Calm your defensiveness, and start with this:

Recognize the "conflict resolution moment"

...when your child wants something you consider unacceptable or you want something your child considers unacceptable.

Engage your "conflict resolution mindset"

By listening to understand and getting creative, together we come up with a resolution that meets both my needs and my child's needs.

Then take these four steps:

1. **Ask about your child's need.**
2. **Explain your own need.**
3. **Brainstorm win-win solutions to meet both needs.**
4. **Jointly identify which options are acceptable to both of you.**

Step 1: Ask about your child's need.

The key is understanding the difference between a "want" and a "need." Wants are ways to satisfy needs. Usually you'll hear an initial request or demand. This is their "want." But they want something for a reason; it satisfies a need. There's almost always more than one way to satisfy a need, not just the initial request. So why does your child want what they say they want? Ask what *need* their want fulfills, and then listen carefully to understand what your child says.

Mom: "This rock concert is over a hundred miles from here! Why is this such a big deal? Can't you guys do something else?"

Daughter: "Everybody's been talking about the concert for months, and all my friends are going. I've got to go."

Mom: "So it means a lot to you to share this with your friends."

Daughter: "Yes!"

Step 2: Explain your own need.

Remember that your initial demand is only one of many possible ways for you to satisfy your need. So think about the need your want satisfies, state it clearly, and then check to be sure you were understood.

Mom: "I hear you. But will you listen to why I have a problem with it?"

Daughter: "Okay..."

Mom: "I want you to have good times, and I know friends are important. But I need to keep you safe until you're old enough to leave home and make your own way in life. The concert is in Pittsburgh, a hundred miles away. At night. The car will be packed with excited teenagers, and whoever is driving will probably be distracted and tired driving home."

Daughter: "We'll be careful. You know my friends. They aren't the wild and crazy type. We'll be all right."

Mom: "I know that's the plan, but I'm not comfortable with all the risk factors."

Daughter: "Oh, Mom, I'll just die if I can't go with them!"

Step 3. Brainstorm win-win solutions to meet both needs.

Without further discussion, critique or justification, encourage your child to brainstorm with you to create a list of new options that will satisfy *both your need and your child's need* at the same time.

Mom: "Honey, I do want you to have fun with your friends, and this rock concert sounds like the best kind of fun. You don't want to be left out when your friends are out having a wonderful time, right?"

Daughter: "Right!"

Mom: "I get that. What I need is to know you're going to be safe, not in harm's way."

Daughter: "I'll be safe."

Mom: "That's what I need. So what I'd like to do is for both of us to step outside the box for a minute and think of some ways that you can have a great time with your friends, and I can be assured it's not a risky situation. Let's think of how we can meet your needs and my needs at the same time."

Daughter: "I can't think of anything."

Mom: "Work with me a little bit. I'll go first. There's lots of cool stuff to do around here. How about you tell your friends about my concerns and suggest something local? We could spend a day at the lake. I'll pay."

Daughter: "I don't like it. They'll go without me."

Mom: "Okay, but now it's your turn. What else might meet both our needs?"

Daughter: "I don't want to do anything else, Mom. Sherry's parents already bought the tickets."

Mom: "Okay, I'll suggest something else. How about I go with you and you let me drive?"

Daughter: "Oh, Mom! They'll think you're a chaperone or something!"

Mom: "Well think of something else. It's your turn."

Daughter: "What if you hire a limo? It would be expensive, but we'd be safe."

Step 4. Jointly identify which options are acceptable to both of you.

Discuss the pros and cons of the creative options and select the one most acceptable to both of you.

Mom: "You know what? That's an interesting suggestion. It does address my concerns. But yes, the expense. I tell you what. How about we check with the other parents. Maybe they'll agree to share the cost. But even if they don't, if it means this much to you, how about we split the cost of the limo? I'll advance you your allowance to cover your half. What do you say?"

Daughter: *Long pause.* "Okay, mom, that works for me."

Mom: "Let's talk with your father and see what he says."

In this process, you don't play the power card. You don't compete to win. And you don't bargain or compromise. You don't give up something to get something. Both parties get what they need.

Tips for optimizing the way you resolve conflict:

- **Self-regulate.** Your signal to shift to conflict resolution is the feeling of wanting to get your own way. If you cringe when you learn what your child wants, keep these feelings to yourself. Instead, exercise patience, consideration and tact in order to listen to understand your child's wants and needs.

- **Get creative.** Rather than automatically standing your ground and getting involved in a power struggle, be open to alternate solutions. Take the brainstorm approach: explore alternate solutions that will meet both your needs and the needs of your child.

- **Take the lead.** When you realize your child wants something you can't live with, recognize that you're the adult in the room. You'll need to be the one to initiate the four steps of win-win creative conflict resolution.

- **Ask for cooperation.** Encourage your child to listen and be creative while searching for solutions.

- **Practice with your spouse.** Spouses have conflicts, too! Take the lead to try the win-win approach to finding a solution that will work for both you and your spouse. Good practice!

- **Use the steps to resolve conflicts between children.** Don't expect kids to be able to use this approach without your help. You can walk them through it, step by step, getting them to be creative about meeting their needs, rather than insisting on their initial demands.

To get your "reps," stay alert for conflict resolution moments, such as when your child:

- Wants to do something you don't want them to do

- Wants more independence

- Wants something you can't afford

- Wants to have fun with friends instead of doing their chores

- Doesn't want to agree to a family guideline

- Has a conflict with a friend or another family member

Does the win-win approach really work? Yes, it does. It has worked every time I've used it in tough conflict situations. I once used the technique to help two executives who had held grudges against each other for fifteen years. In the end, they shook hands and hugged each other. While it's true that some conflicts don't lend themselves to this method, most do.

Imagine the resentment you'll create if you simply lay down the law without making an effort to satisfy your child's needs. When you win and your kid wins, you *grow the bond*.

This chapter in a nutshell:

- **Conflict resolution is not about winning the conflict. It's about finding a way to satisfy both people's needs.**

- **Listen to find out what your child wants, and then ask them about their needs—what their want will do for them.**

- **Explain your need, and then brainstorm alternative ways to satisfy both needs.**

Learn more about conflict resolution:

- Roger Fisher, William Ury and Bruce Patton, *Getting to Yes* (Penguin, 2011)

- Dudley Weeks, *The Eight Essential Steps to Conflict Resolution* (Tarcher-Putnam, 1992)

- Mel Silberman, *PeopleSmart* (Barrett-Koehler, 2000), Skill 6

PART THREE

....

The Path to Mastery

This book focuses on what I consider to be the top 10 communication skills for parents. Its goal is to help you replace dysfunctional behavior patterns with mutually beneficial ones. By now you appreciate that making this effort is a significant undertaking. As Mark Twain said, "Habit is habit and not to be flung out of the window by any man, but coaxed downstairs one step at a time."

I recommend that you work on all 10 skills—one at a time, keeping in mind that mastery is a relative term. Even if you make dramatic progress at first, you can continue to improve a skill throughout your life.

Success is definitely within your reach, if you make a long-term commitment. To stick with it, keep the many payoffs in mind.

"We resist new maneuvers because they make us feel clumsy, awkward and more at risk. But if you want to accelerate your rate of achievement rapidly, you must search out and vigorously employ new behaviors."

Price Pritchett

"Few things are impossible to diligence and skill. Great works are performed not by strength, but perseverance."

Samuel Johnson

14

....

How You Can Continuously Improve Over Time

I wrote this book to help you grow the bond with your child by improving 10 powerful communication skills. I've focused only on this handful of skills because I believe they have the most beneficial impact on the parent-child relationship. It would be daunting to attempt more. If you tried to improve dozens of interpersonal skills, you would soon be overwhelmed.

It's going to be challenging enough to work on these ten. As I affirmed in Chapter 3 ("The Secret to Improving Communication Skills"), you're unlikely to use any of them in the heat of the moment on a busy, tiring day if you haven't established them as your dominant pattern—an automatic, comfortable habit. And the brain cells involved in the skill won't connect into an empowering circuit for the habit from just one successful experience. While each repetition will stimulate the brain cells to wire together and insulate, it will take many reps to finish the job. And this journey will be frustrating, because old habits will sometimes kick in before you've finished wiring your brain for new, more effective ones. Learning from your successes and failures will take time and persistence. You'll need to stay focused on the benefits that come from connecting with your child.

Now that you've read the chapters of Part Two and have familiarized yourself with the skills, you may be asking yourself, *What should I do now? What's the best way to continue improving the way I connect with my child?* The purpose of this chapter is to answer these questions and keep you moving on your learning journey. In these final pages, I'll outline a plan I believe will work to make you a better parent communicator.

In the best case, both parents need to work on improving their parent-child communication skills.

Statistically, more moms than dads read parenting books. This may have to do with one of the important differences between female and male brains: the more robust corpus callosum in the female brain (the bundle of fibers between the left and right sides of the brain) makes it easier for women to communicate their feelings and create relationships.

But both Mom and Dad are partners in the raising of their child to be a happy, successful, independent adult. And effective communication between parent and child is the key, no matter which parent is involved. Ideally, both parents become highly skilled communicators and are on the same page.

So, Dad, if you're the one who found this book, share it with your spouse. And the same for Mom. You can coach and encourage each other as you learn and prepare for your child's adolescence.

If possible, begin improving your skills before your child reaches adolescence.

The second dozen years of growing up are the hardest, both for the parent and the child. It's a whole new ballgame, as they say. Maturing physically and mentally, adolescent children are discovering who they are, learning how the world works, and trying to figure out their place in it. They're pushing for more independence, while parents are trying to instill the maturity and sense of responsibility that will keep them healthy and safe during this time of experimentation.

The whole point of this book is that without effective communication skills, parents' best efforts will sometimes seem to cause more issues than they resolve. So the best-case scenario is that Mom and Dad together proactively begin the work of replacing old habits of relating with improved skills *before* their child reaches puberty.

This doesn't mean that if your child is already a teenager that your efforts to learn new skills will have no effect. Even if there's a history of conflict and hostility, you can begin to change your relationship with your teen by applying the skills described in this book. In short, while it may be ideal to be ready to use these skills with your young "tween," it's never too late to start connecting.

Become more empathetic.

Working on interpersonal skills requires a long-term commitment. Consider how hard it would be to stay the course if there was emotional distance between you and your child, or if you weren't genuinely interested in their life, interests, challenges, and dreams.

To further deepen your sense of compassion, whenever you encounter your child, try to imagine what it's like to be them at that moment: their perceptions, thoughts, feelings, memories, needs, and imaginings. Every person and every child is different. Make it your goal to sense your child's special uniqueness. Your ability to genuinely appreciate who your child is right now will have a positive impact on how you apply the skills.

Practice recognizing your reactive moments.

In the past, you may have had a surge of frustration or anger that led to raising your voice, or worse: toxic questions, put-downs, sarcasm, name-calling, threats, ultimatums, commands, lectures, and so on. If so, you may have felt a twinge of remorse afterward, because you know that reactions like these will not, in the end, help you prepare your child for adulthood. But at the time, in the moment when you "lost your cool," you were probably too upset to be aware that you were "reacting," instead of communicating effectively.

I suggest that before you make a serious project of working on any of the skills, do two things:

- Practice being self-aware in those moments when you feel your emotions rising, when you feel the urge to lash out or play the power card.

- Instead of expressing yourself emotionally, take a deep breath and say or do nothing. Just walk away until you feel calm again.

Doing this a few times will help you build a pattern of self-control, which will set you up for exercising a skill instead, once you're ready to put it into practice.

Focus on improving one skill at a time.

Believe me, doing the work to get good at *one* of the 10 skills is all any busy parent can handle. Like multi-tasking, the failure to focus would be counter-productive. My advice is to work on just one skill, with its subskills and tips for refinement, until you feel so comfortable with it that it becomes second nature. Only then will you get consistent results while trying to improve another skill.

It's also a good idea to focus on one subskill at a time. For example, when learning to be a better listener, I recommend spending time improving the way you feel and express empathy, one of the important elements of listening.

Likewise, once you've become comfortable with the skill, aim for refining your effectiveness. Each chapter suggests "tips," which you can consciously focus on—one at a time—when practicing the skill and learning from these experiences.

Work on becoming a better listener first.

I recommended this approach in Chapter 4 ("Listen to Understand"). Listening is an essential component of each of the other skills. For example, when trying to resolve a conflict, your child will try to give reasons for what they want to do. To discover their core need, you'll need to hear and understand their reasons.

The payoff for being a good listener is huge. Relationships are a two-way street; both you and your child have to make an effort to connect. When your child senses that they're being heard, they'll feel understood, valued, and respected—something kids want and appreciate. They'll feel their effort to open up to you is worth it, that the relationship is satisfying. More than any other skill, listening to understand helps grow the bond between parent and child.

Learn to recognize when to use a skill.

One of the most frustrating aspects of learning a communication skill is realizing that you missed an opportunity to use it. In the previous chapters we identified these opportunities, such as "the listening moment" and "the listening mindset." The descriptions of all the moments and mindsets are summarized in Appendix 2 ("Summary of 'Communication Moments' and 'Communication Mindsets'"). Reviewing these from time to time will help you fix them in your mind.

Practice putting the steps/subskills together in a continuous flow.

While it's an effective learning technique to focus on one step/subskill at a time, your ultimate goal is to get comfortable using all the elements of a skill. Some of them, such as conflict resolution, work best when you apply the steps in sequence. But in real life, your interaction may not follow that order. Your child may skip a step or jump to the desired end result without your help, which is fine. Or you may achieve the connection you hope for using just one aspect of a skill, such as restating expectations when giving feedback. You approach mastery when you have the confidence to go with the flow of the interaction instead of following a procedure lock-step, which might feel awkward and unnatural to both of you.

Practice with everyone.

The focus of this book is to help you connect and grow the bond with your child. But as I've mentioned, these are adult-to-adult skills. They're exactly the same skills that are introduced in leader development and team-building programs. They're the same skills used by professionals such as coaches, mediators, therapists and counselors, who depend on effective communication in their practice. In other words, you can achieve wonderful benefits by using them with your spouse, other family members, friends, or coworkers. In all these relationships, there are countless moments for connecting well. When you express empathy with your mother, the experience helps ingrain the skill for expressing it with your child. When you use the skills to resolve a conflict with your boss, you'll find it easier to do the same thing with your child.

Learn from your mistakes.

When you forget what you should have done or your best effort doesn't go well, ask yourself:

- *What happened? What did I say?*
- *Why did I say it that way?*
- *What affect did this have on the other person?*
- *What can I do next time to get better results?*
- *What's my next step?*

Ask for coaching.

The great thing about having a coach is they hold you accountable, give you feedback, and encourage you. Of course, not every parent can invest in working with a parent coach. That's not what I'm suggesting. I've designed this book to be a coaching resource, and I hope you use it to stay on track with the best practices while encouraging yourself to keep trying.

But a book can't replace a caring individual who can, for example, offer feedback. If you have a spouse, a trusted sibling, a friend, or another parent who is also raising a child, you can spend time sharing stories and frustrations. Instead of giving advice, you can coach each other. You can "listen to understand" and "coach them to think" about problems and solutions. You can share this book with them so you can work on the skills together, holding each other accountable, giving feedback, helping each other learn from experience, and encouraging each other.

If your child has achieved a level of maturity, you can even establish this kind of relationship with them, while the two of you work on becoming better communicators together. Adults need to learn these skills because they weren't taught when they were young. But what if your child acquires them before launching into adult life? I can't image a better scenario for growing the bond.

Be patient and persistent.

Interpersonal skills are complex, and you have to fight through the tendency to fall back on old, comfortable habits. Even if you follow my recommendation to work on one skill at a time, getting comfortable with that one skill could take weeks or months. Skill-building isn't an event; it's a process that requires real-world application, recovering from mistakes, and learning from successes and setbacks—a long series of practical applications that slowly cause the brain cells involved in the skill to wire into a circuit and then insulate with myelin. There's no magic bullet, no special technique, unless you consider "doing the work" the secret sauce. Millions of people have become comfortable with new skills because they persisted in spite of lapses and mistakes.

When your child disappoints you or angers you, recognize your rising emotions. Instead of reacting, just breathe. Calm yourself, forgive your teen, and forgive yourself. Think about which of the skills you can use at the moment, and do your best. If it doesn't go as well as you hoped, learn from what happened. Remember your goal, why you're trying to be a better communicator: to preserve and nurture the bond you have with your child. Stay committed for the long haul. It takes years for a young person to become a young adult. And if it takes years to master these powerful parent communication skills, then you'll be doing it together.

You'll be successful and you'll feel the relationship with your child growing stronger, *if you don't give up.*

Keep trying.

This chapter in a nutshell:

- **Learn to recognize moments when a certain skill will help you.**

- **Work on one skill at a time.**

- **Get good at listening first.**

- **Practice the communication skills with everyone in your life, not just your child.**

- **Learn from your mistakes. Improving a skill is a journey involving successes and shortfalls.**

- **Work past discouragement. Don't give up.**

Learn more about creating new habits:

- James Clear, *Atomic Habits* (Avery-Penguin, 2018)

- Charles Duhigg, *The Power of Habit* (Random House, 2012)

"I think the greatest challenge between child and parent is communication."

Sean Covey

15

....

Your Impact

In Chapter 3 ("The Secret to Improving Communication Skills"), Chapter 14 ("How You Can Continuously Improve Over Time"), and in each of the skill-building chapters in between, I trust that two things have become clear:

- These skills have powerful benefits.
- Shifting from old habits to improved skills requires a long-term effort.

Attending a webinar or following a weeklong "summit" can introduce you to some wonderful ideas. But rewiring the part of your brain that drives these skills will happen only if you apply what you learn for weeks or months—one skill at a time.

This means that improving the skills related to being an effective parent communicator needs to be an aspect of lifelong learning. It also means that your efforts to improve are based on your desire to really connect with your child—to overcome the inherent existential separateness between human beings. With empathy, you can begin to discover the evolving reality of your adult-in-the-making.

The payoff will be amazing.

When you communicate in a way that expresses genuine caring, your child will open up to you and trust you'll be there for them.

When you listen deeply, it demonstrates that you care about your child and what they're trying to say. When you make a habit of asking for their ideas and opinions, it not only stimulates them to become better thinkers and problem-solvers, it's seen as a sign of respect. When you give feedback that encourages, they know you're looking out for their best interests. When you accept feedback graciously, your child will feel safe telling you things you need to hear, instead of withholding their concerns out of fear that you'll react negatively. When you engage in dialogue and try to resolve conflicts creatively, you and your child will appreciate each other more and resolve issues instead of stirring up ill will.

Your child will be inspired to elevate their level of effort.

Every child is developing unique strengths and talents, and it's amazing what they can do *if they want to*. But if they're put off by the way they're treated, if they distrust you, they'll lose confidence that their best efforts will be appreciated. Applying these communication skills will bring out their best.

The communication skills that enrich family relationships are the same skills that can enrich all your relationships.

The skills involved in listening to your child work wonderfully when listening to coworkers, friends and other family members. The kind of affirming and constructive feedback that encourages your child is the best way to give feedback to anyone. The approach to dialogue and resolving conflicts recommended in this book is the classic way to avoid arguments and power struggles in any relationship.

It all starts with someone like you who wants to be more effective with people. It's a process of self-development that never ends, and along the way everyone will be inspired by the way you relate to them.

This chapter in a nutshell:

- **Communicating effectively will inspire your child to perform at their best.**

- **A huge bonus: parent-child communication skills work wonderfully well in all human relationships.**

Learn more about a compassionate approach to parent-child relationships:

- Tim Elmore, *12 Huge Mistakes Parents Can Avoid* (Harvest House, 2014)

- Deborah Gilboa, *Get the Behavior You Want...Without Being the Parent You Hate* (DemosHealth, 2014)

Appendix 1

Summary of Suggested Reading

For readers interested in learning more about skill-building and interpersonal communication, here are some books that have influenced my thinking.

Brown, Neil D. *Ending the Parent-Teen Control Battle* (New Harbinger, 2016).

Clear, James. *Atomic Habits* (Avery-Penguin, 2018).

Coates, Dennis. *How Your Teen Can Grow a Smarter Brain,* 2nd Ed. (First Summit, 2020).

Covey, Stephen R. *The 7 Habits of Highly Effective Families* (Golden, 1997).

Crabb, Larry. *Encouragement: The Unexpected Power of Building Others Up* (Zondervan, 2013).

Crane, Thomas G. *The Heart of Coaching*, 4th Ed. (FTA Press, 2014).

Duhigg, Charles. *The Power of Habit* (Random House, 2012).

Elmore, Tim. *12 Huge Mistakes Parents Can Avoid* (Harvest House, 2014).

Faber, Adele and Elaine Mazlish. *How to Talk So Teens Will Listen & Listen So Teens Will Talk* (HarperCollins, 2006).

Fisher, Roger, with William Ury and Bruce Patton. *Getting to Yes*. (Penguin, 2011).

Folkman, Joe. *Turning Feedback into Change* (Novations, 1996).

Gilboa, Deborah. *Get the Behavior You Want...Without Being the Parent You Hate* (DemosHealth, 2014).

Goldsmith, Marshall. *What Got You Here Won't Get You There* (Hyperion, 2007).

Gordon, Thomas. *Parent Effectiveness Training* (Three Rivers, 2000).

Goulston, Mark. *Just Listen* (AMACOM, 2010).

Healy, Jane M. *How to Have Intelligent and Creative Conversations with Your Kids* (Doubleday, 1992).

Isaacs, William. *Dialogue* (Random House, 2008).

Kaufman, Josh. *The First 20 Hours* (Penguin, 2013).

Marchand, Marie-Eve. *The Spirit of Dialogue in a Digital Age* (Dialogue Publications, 2019).

Maurer, Rick. *Feedback Toolkit* (Productivity Press, 1994).

McKay, Matthew, Martha Davis and Patrick Fanning. *Messages*, 3rd ed. (New Harbinger, 2009).

Rock, David. *Quiet Leadership* (HarperBusiness, 2007).

Silberman, Mel. *PeopleSmart* (Barrett-Koehler, 2000).

Stiffelman, Susan. *Parenting with Presence* (New World, 2015).

Weeks, Dudley. *The Eight Essential Steps to Conflict Resolution* (Tarcher-Putnam, 1992).

Appendix 2

Summary of "Communication Moments" and "Communication Mindsets"

In order to apply communication skills effectively, you must first recognize opportunities to use them and engage the right attitude.

Listen to Understand
(Chapter 4)

Recognize the "listening moment"

...when your child is trying to tell you something you need to hear.

Engage your "listening mindset"

I care about my child's problems, thoughts, and feelings. Something is going on with them right now, and I want to know what it is. So rather than react negatively or assume I understand, I check what I'm hearing.

Coach Your Child to Think
(Chapter 5)

Recognize the "thinking moment"

...when you can encourage your child to do their own thinking, rather than give them the answer or solution.

Engage your "thinking mindset"

I ask open-ended questions that encourage my child to practice thinking: understanding, reasoning, evaluating, problem-solving, decision-making, goal-setting, planning, and organizing.

Guide Learning from Experience
(Chapter 6)

Recognize the "learning moment"

...when something significant has happened, and your child can learn from it.

Engage your "learning mindset"

I ask open-ended questions that encourage my child to analyze what happened so they can improve the way they approach problems in the future.

Get Buy-in for Expectations
(Chapter 7)

Recognize the "buy-in moment"

...when faced with a goal, milestone or task, and you expect specific effort or results from your child.

Engage your "buy-in mindset"

My child is more motivated to accomplish a difficult objective if they own it, and so I ask for their input to help frame it.

Offer Encouragement
(Chapter 8)

Recognize the "encouragement moment"

...when you notice that something has happened to cause your child to be discouraged.

Engage your "encouragement mindset"

My child sometimes doesn't bounce back from adversity right away. I remind them of their strengths, what's possible, and that I want to support them.

Express Appreciation
(Chapter 9)

Recognize the "appreciation moment"

...when you notice that your child has done something well, made a special effort, or achieved something outstanding.

Engage your "appreciation mindset"

I notice when my child has done their best and affirm them for their effort.

Give Feedback Constructively
(Chapter 10)

Recognize the "feedback moment"

...when your child's behavior has come up short and you want to inspire them to do better.

Engage your "feedback mindset"

When I'm not happy with my child's behavior, I share how I feel about it in a positive, encouraging way.

Accept Feedback Graciously
(Chapter 11)

Recognize the "accept feedback graciously moment"

...when your child has given you feedback and you want to encourage this kind of input in the future.

Engage your "accept feedback graciously mindset"

I ask for feedback, and when my child gifts me with it in any form, I listen without reacting, thank them, and follow up with an effort to change my behavior.

Engage in Dialogue
(Chapter 12)

Recognize the "dialogue moment"

...when you realize that you don't agree with your child's point of view.

Engage your "dialogue mindset"

My child and I may disagree, but we're entitled to our opinions. Without trying to win an argument, I keep an open mind and make an effort to learn why my child has this opinion.

Resolve Conflict Creatively
(Chapter 13)

Recognize the "conflict resolution moment"

...when your child wants something you consider unacceptable or you want something your child considers unacceptable.

Engage your "conflict resolution mindset"

By listening to understand and getting creative, together we come up with a resolution that meets both my needs and my child's needs.

Appendix 3

Learn from Experience

Experience can be a great teacher, but if you don't think about what happened, you may not learn from it. Whether a success or a disappointment, to capture the lesson, ask yourself these open-ended questions:

1. **What happened?** The details of an event need to be recalled in order to make sense of them. What was the sequence of events? What did you do? How did others react? How do you feel about it?

2. **Why did you handle it this way?** Things happen for a reason. To imagine a better way to handle a situation like this, try to understand why things occurred the way they did. What were you thinking? What helped or hindered? What led to the outcome?

3. **What were the consequences?** Appreciating the impact of what happened creates the motivation to handle situations like this more effectively. Benefits? Costs? Problems? Resolutions?

4. **How would you handle a similar situation in the future?** What did you learn from this experience? What basic principles? How are you going to apply the lesson?

5. **What are your next steps?** What will you do in the next day or two to set you up for implementing this learning?

You have permission to make a copy of this page.

Appendix 4

Life Skills

When a child becomes an adult, they'll have to handle the same problems and challenges you deal with every day. With some exceptions, learning life skills aren't the main focus of their formal education. With strong communication skills, parents are better equipped to involve their children in age-appropriate chores, projects and responsibilities. With few life skills, young adults may have to struggle to catch up later. I'm sure there are things you wish you had learned when you were younger.

As you help them prepare for life, you can refer to this list of general "life skills," each of which can be broken down into specific subskills:

Etiquette
Grooming
Health/hygiene
Nutrition, meal planning
Food preparation
Fitness
Safety
Sexual health
Device maintenance
Vehicle operation
DIY/home repairs
Using tools
Interpersonal communication
Building relationships
Critical thinking/creativity
Self-discipline/regulation

Time management
Money management
Problem-solving
Decision-making
Planning
Organization
Project management
Leadership
Researching
Learning
Writing
Public speaking
Mindfulness/meditation

Appendix 5

Thinking Skills

In the adult world, advantages are awarded to individuals who have superior minds, people who have displayed an impressive array of thinking skills. Your ability to communicate effectively will create opportunities to encourage your child to become a better thinker. School teachers excel at introducing concepts and facts. While a few may also stimulate their students to *think* about the subject matter, you can play a key role in this aspect of your child's development. I devote a whole chapter in my book, *How Your Teen Can Grow a Smarter Brain*, to guiding parents to ask questions that stimulate their kids to do their own thinking.

A few of these thinking skills are included in the list of Life Skills (Appendix 4). Here's a more complete list:

Understanding meaning	Recognizing logic fallacies
Forming concepts	Assessing worth/quality
Sensing knowledge gaps	Judging right and wrong
Integrating new knowledge	Foreseeing consequences
Listening to understand	Interpreting nonverbals
Drawing conclusions	Exercising empathy
Questioning assumptions	Evaluating own actions
Considering points of view	Considering intuition
Learning from experience	Managing emotions
Analyzing cause and effect	Controlling impulsiveness
Reasoning	Identifying problems
Checking facts	Imagining new possibilities

Solving problems
Evaluating possible actions
Making decisions
Setting goals
Establishing priorities

Planning
Organizing resources
Initiating tasks
Directing attention/focus
Managing time

Appendix 6

Core Strengths

Being a better communicator will make it easier to encourage your child to get involved in activities that will make them stronger as a person. Young people need practice doing the hard things. When they work at chores, projects, sports, hobbies, or money-making activities, they'll be challenged. These are opportunities to prepare for situations they'll face as adults. While they're involved in these activities, you can listen to them talk about their experiences and help them learn from them.

To help you understand the behavior patterns they could be forming, here's a list of core strengths young people can build during youth and beyond.

Personal Growth
1. Self-development
2. Self-awareness
3. Self-esteem
4. Self-confidence
5. Perseverance
6. Optimism
7. Acceptance
8. Courage
9. Gratitude
10. Self-discipline

Relationships
1. Fairness
2. Loyalty
3. Tolerance
4. Trust
5. Cooperation
6. Compassion
7. Honesty
8. Integrity
9. Open-mindedness
10. Service

Performance/Work Ethic

1. Initiative
2. Patience
3. Passion
4. Creativity
5. Focus
6. Commitment
7. Effort
8. Excellence
9. Thoroughness
10. Accountability

Leadership

1. Awareness
2. Responsibility
3. Empowerment
4. Decisiveness
5. Vision
6. Flexibility
7. Proactivity
8. Rationality
9. Intuition
10. Composure

Acknowledgements

My thinking about parent-child communication has been heavily influenced by the work of other experts in this field. I'm reminded of what Isaac Newton said: "If I have seen further than others, it is by standing upon the shoulders of giants." My introduction to communication skill development happened in 1976. I was a major in the Army, chief of human resources for the 32d Air Defense Command, which was in charge of all surface-to-air missile sites in Germany during the Cold War. At the time, drug use among our soldiers was a big problem, and in advance of creating a program for commanders to deal with it, I attended a month-long course that introduced me to group facilitation, listening, feedback, and other skills. It was there that I discovered the book, *P.E.T.—Parent Effectiveness Training*, by Dr. Thomas Gordon. The notion that one could learn a few powerful skills to become a better communicator and more effective parent was a revelation to me. It literally changed my life.

After I retired from the Army in 1987, I co-founded Performance Support Systems, a company that creates brain-based learning technologies to help adults in the workplace improve their leader and team interpersonal skills. Ten years ago my study of how the brain develops, learns, and functions led me to a passionate interest in child and adolescent development. Over the years, the work of experts in communication and parenting contributed greatly to my understanding: Jane Healy, Mark Goulston, Haim Ginot, Stephen Covey, Marshall Goldsmith, Michael Gurion, Deborah Gilboa, Robert Bolton, Madelyn

Burley-Allen, David Walsh, Neil Brown, Tim Elmore, Laura Markham, Matthew McKay, Mel Silberman, Marie-Eve Marchand, Adele Faber, and Elaine Mazlish.

This book is heavily influenced by my previous book, *Connect with Your Team*, which I co-authored with Meredith Bell. For over 30 years our approach to helping adults learn communication skills grew out of the ideas and recommendations from our association with consultants and coaches: Rick and Susan Stamm, Elizabeth Fried, Bud Cummings, Mark Hinderliter, Mark Spool, Dennis LaMountain, Camille Harris, Jeff Backal, Graham Da Costa, Janyne Peek Emsick, Larry Brower, and Alice Dendinger.

During the writing of this book I benefited from valuable suggestions and encouragement from parent coaches, family therapists, parenting authors, and parents, who read early drafts: Thomas Kersting, Sam Renick, Dennis Trittin, Lynne Kenney, Elisabeth Stitt, Tyse Kimball, Kevin Thompson, Frank Thompson, Cath Hakanson, Alexis Rodegerdts, Joanie Connell, and Karen McFadyen.

As with previous books, I'm indebted to Kathleen Scott and Paula Schlauch for their careful reading, editing, set-up, and unwavering support.

About the Author

Dr. Denny Coates is an expert in parent-child communication and adolescent brain development. He is the author of several books and hundreds of articles for parents. His two latest books, *Connect with Your Kid: Mastering the Top 10 Parent-Child Communication Skills* and *Parents Coaching Parents*, provide a practical, step-by-step approach that helps parents build a bond with their child that lasts a lifetime. You can find information about his books and other resources at DrDennyCoates.com.

He is the father of two grown sons, and he lives with his wife, Kathleen Scott, near San Antonio, Texas.

Website & blog:
https://DrDennyCoates.com

LinkedIn: DrDennyCoates

Twitter: @DrDennyCoates

Denny is available as a podcast guest and as a speaker at corporate or association events.

Quantity sales. Special discounts are available on quantity purchases by corporations, associations and others. For details, contact us at info@growstrongleaders.com or 757-656-4765.

www.ingramcontent.com/pod-product-compliance
Lightning Source LLC
LaVergne TN
LVHW051507080426
835509LV00017B/1959